Maybe He's Just an Asshole

Ditch Denial, Embrace Your Worth, and Find True Love!

by

Halle Kaye & Sophie Stone

ISBN: 1475039484
ISBN-13: 978-1475039481

A caveat:

This is not intended to be an "anti-man" or "man-hating" book. As one reviewer pointed out, we use the term "asshole" in a playful, snarky, tongue-in-cheek kind of way to refer to men who are a waste of your time. It's precisely because we believe there are so many wonderful men out there that we want to help you ditch the bad ones fast!

Visit us on the web!

www.TheAholeBook.com

On the site, you'll find links to us on Facebook and Twitter, and our email address.

CONTENTS

Introduction   1

Chapter One – The Guy Who Sucks at   6
Communication
    He's Technology-Challenged   6
    He Goes MIA When Life Gets Busy   8
    He Text-Fights   12

Chapter Two – The Guy Who's Hot and Cold   16
    Up, Down: He Cools Off Between Dates   16
    He's Baaaaaaack: The Ex Who Won't Leave   18
    He's a Serial Break-Upper   22
    He's Better When He Hits the Bottle   25
    He Wants a Fuck Buddy, Not a Girlfriend   27

Chapter Three – The Guy Who's Conflicted   32
About You
    He Believes You Have a Shelf Life   32
    He Wants a Skinny Bitch   35
    He's Team Jesus. You're Team Buddha   38

Chapter Four – The Guy Who's Just Not   42
Ready to Commit
    He Wants to Test-Drive You For a While   42
    First
    He's Not Ready to Retire His Bachelor Status   45
    He's Stuck in a Professional Rut   48
    He's Too Busy to Get Hitched   52
    He's Nursing a Broken Heart   55

Chapter Five – The Guy Who's Not Trustworthy   58

    He's Prince Charming   58

    He's a Late-Night Texter   61

    He's a Chronic Cheater   64

    He Takes You to Parties, Not Dates   67

    He Overlaps Girlfriends   70

    He Has Endless Phone Excuses   73

    He's Got a Dirty Little Secret: You   76

Chapter Six – The Guy Who's Insecure   78

    He Needs to be Alpha Dog   78

    He Hits Below the Belt   81

    He Can't Stop Talking About Other Women   84

    He's a Control Freak   87

Chapter Seven – The Guy Who Has an Unhealthy Relationship to Sex   90

    He Won't Glove His Love   90

    He Won't Stop When It Hurts   93

    He Thinks His Morning Dry Hump is Foreplay   95

    He's a Premature Sexter   97

    He's a Porn Dog   99

    He Wants to Double His Pleasure   102

    He's Obs-ASS-ed   104

Conclusion   108

Index   110

INTRODUCTION

We love men. And there are some amazing men out there.

But if you're a woman, you know a good guy isn't easy to find. Because let's face it:

The manscape is a minefield of assholes.

So many guys who seem like great catches are actually just assholes walking around in disguise. If you're not careful, you could end up wasting precious time, if not your entire life, with a bad dude. You have to get good at differentiating the diamonds from the dirt.

Complicating things even further, many of the dating rules we've been following suggest that it's a man's world and we're just living in it. Somehow, nearly all the romantic rules of engagement we've been taught were written from the perspective of the penis — they're focused on how we should behave so that a man will want us and how to determine whether he does.

Think about it.

When a guy doesn't treat us well, we often blame ourselves. We might think, *hmmm, maybe he's just not that into me,* as if we weren't hot/smart/funny/cool enough to deserve better from him. And we'll often agonize about how to get him to like us more, only to end up feeling embarrassed for ourselves as we behave more and more pathetically.

If you've dated your share of unsatisfying guys, you know how toxic those relationships can be. They can be deeply frustrating, make us feel crazy, totally waste our time, cause us tremendous pain, destroy our self-esteems and diminish any hope we have that there's a great guy out there for us.

There has to be another way.

And there is. That's what this book is about. It's about taking the power back. It's about understanding and identifying what you need from a guy so you can evaluate the men you meet against that criteria. Not the other way around. It's no longer about whether he's into you; it's about whether *you're* into *him*. This may not sound like a radical idea but trust us, it is absolutely life-altering.

So, ladies, new rule: If a guy doesn't give you what you need, don't doubt your own desirability – doubt his.

When you start truly understanding the power of this approach and how to apply it, amazing things will happen. You'll realize you have a lot more control in life and love than you thought. You'll become more confident, more attractive, and exponentially more magnetic. And the way men respond to you will blow your mind. It's crazy.

Are you ready to approach dating not from a place of weakness and desperation but from a place of strength and power? If so, read on…

This book will help you:

<u>Ditch denial</u> so you don't end up wasting time with the wrong guys;

<u>Embrace Your Worth</u> because the more you believe you deserve, the more you'll demand, and the more you'll get; and

<u>Find true love</u>, which will happen more quickly as you begin to approach dating from the perspective of your strongest self – the sexiest, most confident version of yourself who knows what she wants and deserves, and doesn't settle for less.

The best part: No rules, games or bitchiness required.

We'll help you to get in touch with your best self so that you can become more successful not just in romance, but in your entire life. Because the fact is that you will only find an amazing man when you act like, and truly believe, that an amazing man is what you deserve.

Maybe He's Just An Asshole is broken up into seven chapters, each covering a different type of bad guy.

Each chapter includes:

Anecdotal stories illustrating common dating scenarios.* We assess each situation by identifying the important issues, discussing the motivations of the guy involved, and explaining why he's probably an asshole.

Asshole ratings. Using our highly scientific Asshole Meter, we assign the guy in every story an asshole rating on a scale of 1 to 10 and provide an explanation for the rating. A low asshole rating (6 or below) suggests the guy may have asshole-ish tendencies, but he also just may be a douchebag or a loser. A high asshole rating (7 or above) suggests that the guy is almost certainly an asshole.

Principles on how to become your strongest self. Every story ends with one to three 60-second pep talks designed to stop your mental shitshow, re-adjust your attitude and put you on the path to finally getting what you deserve from the men in your life. Consider them mini pick-me-ups when you need to set yourself straight about asshole behavior.

So, are you ready to become your strongest self? Let's get started!

*Please note that these stories are fictional, partially based on our own experiences and those of our friends.

CHAPTER ONE

The Guy Who Sucks at Communication

He's Technology-Challenged

The guy I've been seeing for four months, David, has an annoying habit: he often takes hours to respond to my texts and calls or just ignores them altogether. It's not a huge deal because I know he likes me – he usually reaches out to hang out at least two or three times a week – but I still don't like that he's not responsive when I initiate communication. I've brought this up with him and he just sweet talks his way out of it saying he's just bad at that stuff. Should I let him off the hook or push him to be better about this?

David says he's just "bad at that stuff." But what does that mean? Is he bad at typing? Are the tips of his fingers unusually large and blunt such that using a keyboard is a particularly arduous task for him? Does he have trouble figuring out which end of the phone to speak into? Or is he mentally challenged to such a degree that your flirtatious little notes confuse him?

Because if David can type, and a simple "Hey babe, will I see you tonight?" doesn't boggle his mind, then he's just an asshole. <u>Not</u> regularly ignoring someone you're dating, or seeing, or even friends with, is common courtesy and David apparently has no manners.

Bottom line: As a boyfriend, David is selfish and lazy. All David has to do to make you happy is push a bunch of buttons but, nope, he won't do that for you. So, when David says he's "bad at that stuff," what he really means is that he's bad at doing something that he's just not in the mood for, even if it hurts you. He means he's bad at treating you with respect because that takes too much energy. He means he's bad at being a nice guy because, well, he's just an asshole.

And the Asshole Meter says:

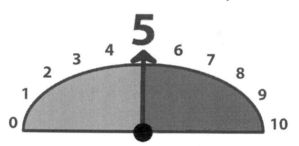

BECAUSE COMMON COURTESY IS NEVER OPTIONAL

Recognize bullshit when you see it. If your guy gives you a lame excuse for some bad behavior, don't roll over and accept it, thinking, "Maybe he'll change" or "At least I have someone." That's your weakest self rationalizing someone else's baggage. And your weakest self shouldn't be making your decisions, running your life. Instead, take a step back and get in touch with your strongest self. She's the voice of truth in the background, your best friend who loves you, wants the best for you, and tells it like it is. If you think your guy might be playing you for a fool, consult with your strongest self. Ask her what she thinks and let her be your guide. She'll speak the truth.

Never negotiate the basics. There are things you can compromise on with your guy: rom coms versus action flicks, his place or yours, missionary versus cowgirl. That's normal and healthy. There are other things, however, that should never be up for debate, such as feeling heard, valued, supported, safe and equal. Any relationship that forces you to settle for less will likely fail or leave one or both of you feeling miserable. Your strongest self understands this. She's searching for a healthy, productive relationship and senses when something important might be missing. When a guy isn't meeting her basic needs, she doesn't talk herself into believing she's the one who's got the problem or go into denial so she can stay with him. No – she moves on, gracefully. Because your strongest self is no fool. She realizes her worth. She knows with absolute certainty that there's a better guy out there for her and *that's* who she wants.

****

He Goes MIA When Life Gets Busy

My boyfriend, Jonathan, is a great catch. He's super successful, handsome, and smart, and the sex is mind-blowing. We've been seeing each other for a year and things are pretty good. The one issue I have is that he disappears on me when he gets super busy or travels. So, a couple of times a month, I won't hear from him for a few days. And every few weeks, he leaves town for several days and, again – silence. One time, he was in Asia for eight days on business and managed to e-mail me only once. I'm pretty low-maintenance and understand that he has a busy job, but shouldn't he be able to call or text every couple of days?

Jonathan isn't a catch. He's just an asshole disguised in catch's clothing.

We have no idea why Jonathan doesn't reach out to you when he's busy. We do know that there's no such thing as being "too busy" to send a short note or make a quick call to your girlfriend when you can't see her for days on end. Good men manage to do it all the time. (Exceptions include brain surgeons, members of Seal Team 6, and astronauts currently on mission.)

Who knows — maybe Jonathan's just not that into you. Or perhaps he doesn't know any better. The "why" doesn't matter as much as the "what." And what he is, is an asshole. We say, toss that catch back in the water.

A man as "smart" as Jonathan surely understands that it's not acceptable to fall off the grid, leaving your partner in the dark. He should take a few seconds to reach out to you. And if he doesn't like you enough to do that, the answer is simple: He shouldn't be with you, wasting your time, making up weak (and dare we say, uncreative) excuses for himself, getting his needs fulfilled, without fulfilling yours.

So, we suggest you break up with super-successful Jonathan. If he asks why, tell him that he's not very successful at being a boyfriend, but he's got this asshole thing nailed. Kudos, Jonathan!

And the Asshole Meter says:

BECAUSE HIDE AND SEEK IS A CHILD'S GAME

Send it back, if it's not what you ordered. Your strongest self is your best advocate. She watches out for you and makes sure you don't get trampled. If you went to Starbucks and ordered a Tall Decaf Caramel Soy Latte and, instead, were served a regular drip coffee, you'd send it back, right? "Um, Mr. Barista," you'd say, "This isn't what I asked for." Similarly, if your guy's behavior doesn't match what you ordered, let him know. Don't whine, nag, get angry, become the victim, or make a scene. Politely state the issue and ask it to be addressed — as if he just made a mistake and, now that he knows better, of course, he'll fix it.

"David," you'd say, "I've been wanting to talk to you about something. You never call me when you're busy or away ... What's that about?" (And then, smile.)

He'll likely say something like, "Oh, yeah, oooh that ... I'm sorry. It's just so hard to find the time when things get crazy or if I'm traveling, you know? I just get so caught up in everything. But you know that doesn't mean anything, right?" (As he strokes your arm.)

"Hmmm. Okay," you reply. "Yeah ... I understand. Only thing is that I kinda need my guy to be better about that. If you can't be, that's totally fine. But, if that's the case, I don't think this is going to work out. Sorry!" (Smile.)

Does the above sound unrealistic to you? We hope not. Because that's how a woman who trusts her needs and judgment would behave: if a guy was doing something that caused her anxiety, frustration, or pain, she would ask him to change his behavior and if he refused, she would read that as a red flag and leave.

But that's not what many of us would do. Many of us would ask a guy to change his behavior and, even if he refused, we would stick around, trying to convince ourselves that what he was doing wasn't that bad or that we'll get him to change eventually. That's because once we decide we like a guy, we often become our weaker selves, afraid to be without him. Instead, we should stay strong, in touch with our reasons for wanting a partner in the first place, and honest with ourselves if the man before us isn't living up to our standards.

Don't be distracted by the package. Get your head out of the gutter, ladies — we're not referring to *that* package. We're referring to the list of attributes that often make us think a guy is a "great" catch: a great job, a great pad, a great body, a great family, a great set of moves in bed... Yeah, we'd think he's pretty damn great, too, as long as he's also a great guy. And the measure of a man's greatness is determined only by how you feel when you're with him, and what energy he brings to your life. In moments of weakness, it's easy to be tempted by what looks good on paper... Fortunately, though, your strongest self knows better. Put her in charge and soon you'll find yourself with an amazing guy whose reality matches the pitch.

****

He Text-Fights

Every time my boyfriend, Jamie, gets mad about something, he doesn't bring it up when we're together — he shuts down, acts strange, and then texts me later to tell me that he's upset. If I call him to hash it out, he won't answer, forcing me to have the conversation on text, which is really hard. Often, silly disagreements turn into huge fights because we've misunderstood each other. We've discussed this — he admits that I'm actually pretty easy to talk to — and he'll be better for about a month but then the same thing happens again. I need him to stop trying to solve our problems on text. What's his deal and how do I fix it?

Jamie's deal is that he's passive aggressive. And kind of a pussy. And while he's not earned the full-blown asshole title, we're confident he's on his way to becoming one.

Jamie has the conflict management skills of a little boy. He's afraid of having a real-time grown-up discussion where he has to look into your face and be accountable for his feelings and opinions in the moment. He'd much rather voice (or type) his concerns from a distance, allowing him to be far less reasonable and giving you very little room to plead your case, causing both of you unnecessary frustration.

Sadly, Jamie's not going to change. A person's style of handling conflict doesn't suddenly evolve over night; it's pretty hard-wired, which means that your relationship will become more dysfunctional over time. He'll continue not being straightforward about what's bothering him, your disagreements will increasingly spiral out of control, and eventually, one or both of you will be miserable, needing your now-toxic relationship to end.

The good news: You're not dating a total asshole.

The bad news: If you stay with him, you will be.

And the Asshole Meter says:

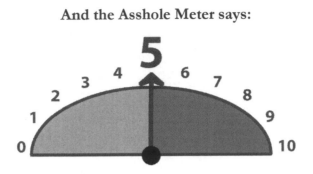

BECAUSE ADULT RELATIONSHIPS REQUIRE ADULT BEHAVIOR

Date men, not boys. A healthy adult relationship is only possible between mature adults. But we get it — it sucks to be alone and when you find a guy who's halfway decent, it seems perfectly fine to accept his childish behavior. After all, no one's perfect. So, you look the other way when he argues like a teenager, refuses to accept responsibility for his choices, or avoids discussing each other's emotions and needs. Unfortunately, you're taking the bullet for his stunted emotional growth. Your strongest self, on the other hand, doesn't settle for that. Not only would she refuse to date someone so immature, she can't even remain attracted to him. She needs and desires a man. Only a man can meet her where she lives mentally, emotionally, and spiritually, and that's what matters to her above all else.

Remember that men are "as is." People generally don't change unless they *reeaally* want to change *and* they undertake a sustained effort to create the change they desire. Without both of those things, which are rarely found together, nothing moves forward — everything stays the same. So, in most instances, a guy who's exhibiting unhealthy patterns in his relationship is not going to change. He may act differently for a few days or weeks —after his partner has demanded it, for example — but he'll generally revert back to his natural baseline. Your strongest self understands this. She doesn't pretend that just because a guy improves slightly over a short period of time, he's become a new and improved version of himself. She realizes that chronic bad behavior generally stems from some pretty messed up values and principles. And you don't need to be a shrink to know that the core of who someone is doesn't shift over night. So, she pays close attention to the issues that bother her, honestly asks herself if they're red flags, and if they are, she moves on. Because there's always something better than an asshole.

CHAPTER TWO
The Guy Who's Hot and Cold

Up, Down: He Cools Off Between Dates

I met Alex a few weeks ago at a party and we hooked up. It was a fabulous night but then I didn't hear from him for a week. I reluctantly saw him again and we had another awesome night. And then ... silence for five days. I went out with him a third time — mostly because his texts are so nice when he finally does get in touch — but then, the icy front moved in again. This time for six days! This has now happened five times and the hot/cold thing is driving me insane. What is that about? My friends keep saying he's just not that into me, but he seems to really like me when we're together. I swear, you'd think we were a couple if you saw us. Could my friends be right??

Um, seriously? Who cares if Alex is into you?

Think about it. This guy is all over the place. Up. Down. Left. Right. He's completely impulse and mood driven. If he wants to see you, he will. If he doesn't, he forgets you exist. And when you tell him enough is enough, he says whatever it takes to change your mind.

Wow. Alex has a fantastic deal. And it's on his terms. His lowlife moves are straight from the Asshole

Handbook.

Men know that women are crazy tolerant when we think a guy is into us. And, sadly, there are a lot of men who have no qualms taking advantage of that by acting like they like us more than they do. Their goal: *to distract us from the fact that they're doing the absolute bare minimum to keep us in play.*

They can be cunning. So you need to be smart.

Next time Alex's warm front moves in, temper the heat with your own chill factor. Guys like Alex don't need a warning, they need to get iced out.

And the Asshole Meter says:

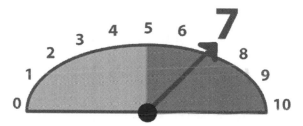

BECAUSE ERRATIC NEVER TURNS INTO DEPENDABLE

Expect to be a priority, not an option. Whenever you're dating someone, ask yourself if he makes you feel like a priority. The answer will come quickly and straight from your gut, so be prepared for the truth. If the answer is "no," then you're just an option, a la Alex, and you've clearly been letting your insecurities take over. Kick your weak ass out of the driver's seat and let your strongest self — the one who doesn't let herself be on call for anyone — take the wheel. Remember: Keep your expectations sky high and your tolerance for bullshit at zero.

Stop wondering whether he's into you. Men can be confusing. It's only natural that we question what's happening in our relationships with them. That's okay. But we should ask the *right* questions. Instead of pondering does he like me, is he into me, does he love me, does he want me, focus on what you need and whether you're getting it. A guy being into you isn't a giant magic eraser for his bad behavior. Your strongest self gets this very fundamental fact. If he doesn't call for a week, she doesn't think, "Oh, maybe he digs me so who cares if he ignores me sometimes." Your strongest self doesn't make decisions based on whether some guy is into her, pretends he's into her, or claims to be into her. She doesn't care about anything other than whether the man she's with is doing everything he can *to make her want him.* End of story.

****

He's Baaaaaack: The Ex Who Won't Leave

My ex-boyfriend Jeff broke up with me six months ago. As devastated as I was, I decided I wouldn't argue. I refused to be that girl. So, I moved on. But he hasn't. He calls and texts every few weeks saying he misses me and needs to see me. I never reach out to him but I do reply when he writes me, just out of curiosity. Of course, when that happens, we always end up in bed. But, I figure, what's the harm? I am dating other guys. I just don't want to slam the door shut on Jeff because there's obviously a part of him that still loves me. And maybe us seeing each other every now and then will make him want to come back, right?

Wrong.

We give you a point for not calling him. But we deduct 20 points for you *wanting* to call him, and 100 points for you sleeping with him.

If there were a Boy Scouts for assholes, Jeff would've earned a badge. Why? He masterfully downgraded his girlfriend to a booty call. He's somehow finagled himself out of standard boyfriend duties — date nights, backrubs, and midnight tampon runs — but still regularly gets to have sex with you! Bravo.

Jeff is not unable to move on. Nor does he need to step it up to win you back. After all, you've made it so easy for him to come and go as he pleases! Jeff now gets to be single, date like a single dude, and play in your sheets without being accountable to you for anything. Convincing him to go back to the way it was isn't even a remote possibility.

And let's be clear: The person who hasn't moved on is you. Although you're not initiating contact, you know he'll be in touch. And you look forward to that. When you do see each other, it unquestionably means a lot more to you than it does to him. While he's using you for sex, you're using sex to reignite his interest in you. While he's out there hitting on other girls, a part of you is plotting how to get him back.

It's a little pathetic. Sorry – just sayin.

And Jeff knows you haven't fully moved on. How? Because you haven't. Men smell weakness in a woman like sharks smell blood. And weakness isn't hot. It's just easy to exploit, which is what Jeff is doing.

If you can't admit it, you can't change it so, face the facts — you're stuck. You miss him. You're excited when he texts you. You love it when he sleeps over. You're sad when he leaves. You wait for him to return. You hope you get back together.

Reality check: That won't happen. Jeff is an asshole. Move on. There's a better man out there once you start acting like a better woman and get off this awful roller-coaster.

And the Asshole Meter says:

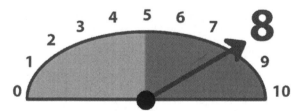

BECAUSE COMING BACK WITHOUT A COMMITMENT IS JUST TAKING ADVANTAGE

Snuff out old flames. Your ex is your ex because

he doesn't want to be with you. If he did, he would be your boyfriend. When you still have feelings for an ex, it's easy to allow yourself to keep hanging on. You convince yourself that it's okay to see him because you've moved on, you're dating other people, you're open to someone new, and you're only keeping the door open for him *just in case*. Those are lies. The truth is you're emotionally stuck. If you're interacting with your ex — whether by phone, in bed or over a cocktail — you're not over him. And it's important for you to acknowledge that so you can address the real issue: you're somehow okay spending time with a man who doesn't really want to be with you, except for a random night here and there.

Your strongest self wouldn't stand for this. Next time Mr. Why-Buy-The-Cow-When-I-Get-The-Milk-For-Free texts, "I miss you. What are you up to tonight?", do what she'd do: Smile smugly to yourself, knowing that some small part of him still wants you. Reply, "Nice to hear from you. Hope all is well!" And then throw on your hottest dress, highest heels, and strut head held high out the door for a fabulous night. Ex not included.

Don't be a sitting duck. Men are hunters. They thrive on the thrill of the chase. So it makes sense that one of the least attractive things to a guy is a woman who won't walk away no matter how proudly he waves his asshole flag. She puts herself in a holding pattern, accepting what little he offers. Your strongest self doesn't pause her life, waiting for her soul to be fed someone else's crumbs. The need to be valued and treated with respect is central to who she is. This gives her the power to walk away from a less-than-stellar relationship or an ex with ulterior motives. Her vibrant self-determination, rock-solid confidence and absolute refusal to take crap is captivating. And it's this highly charged magnetism that will eventually attract the right man.

****

He's a Serial Break-Upper

Noah and I have been on again off again for three years. Basically, he breaks up with me and then, a few weeks or months later, he comes back, saying he can't live without me. When I ask him why he ended things in the first place, I usually get some variation of "Oh, I'm just an idiot" or "I'm scared of commitment" or "I'm trying to grow up." It's infuriating, but at the same time, I love him and I can see the pain he feels without me. Right now, we've been back together for three months and I'm scared because I can sense that I'm losing him again. What can I do to keep him from breaking up with me again?

You're like one of those ladies from the 1800s who used to have to sit around a freezing log cabin by herself for weeks at a time, hoping no outlaws would show up and steal her honor as she waited for her man to return home with a couple of nickels and some dried coyote meat.

Except your situation is not nearly as good. Because

your man is not risking his life for your survival (unless you left that part out of your letter). Frankly, it sounds like he's just an asshole who leaves for no good reason, and then returns with nothing but his needs.

Newsflash: Noah is not busting through a box of tissues every night, listening to Adele, and staring at your picture. Noah is out there canvassing the big, wide world living his life (read: screwing around) and doing his man thang while you're sitting at home in limbo, waiting like a prairie wife.

If Noah looks like he's struggling when he's asking you to take him back, it's only because he's a bad actor. The truth: He's horny, lonely, bored or all of the above and you're available. He really couldn't care less about you except to the extent that you service him.

Who knows if Noah will be a better guy when he grows up? What's clear, however, is that he won't be a better guy to you. Sure, men break up with women and then get back together with them and live happily ever after, but that never happens when the girl is a pushover. Because that girl's not hot. And unfortunately, you're her.

And the Asshole Meter says:

BECAUSE IT'S NOT THAT HARD TO MAKE UP YOUR MIND

Look forward, not back. Breaking up is hard to do unless you're being your strongest self. Sure, it's a little disappointing when another relationship bites the dust and it's normal to harbor some nostalgia for the good times. But your strongest self knows that, more than anything, this is your opportunity to find the right guy. She understands that, if he left you once, he's the wrong guy. And if he keeps leaving you and coming back, he's just an asshole. And what's the point of crying over that?

Recalibrate. Whenever you're in a dysfunctional relationship — one that doesn't make you feel happy, healthy, and satisfied most of the time — pause and ask yourself why you're still in it. It may seem like an obvious question, but so few of us ask it. For some reason, we chicks, once we decide we like a guy, stick around. Come hell or high water. We don't budge. It's as if we want him, above all else, and in order to keep him, we'll lie to ourselves, drop our expectations, try to

change him, convince ourselves we're happy —
anything other than cut him out of our lives because
that's just too hard. Your strongest self, on the other
hand, regularly asks herself if the guy she's dating helps
her be the strongest, happiest version of herself or
holds her back. She reflects honestly on how he makes
her feel and doesn't entertain denial. After all, she's
trying to be her own best advocate, not her own worst
enemy.

****

He's Better When He Hits the Bottle

*I've been dating Matt for a few months. I really like him,
but I've noticed that we don't really connect unless he's had
a couple of drinks. When he's a little buzzed, he makes me
laugh, opens up about his life and becomes really sweet and
affectionate. The rest of the time, like if we're just hanging
out at his house or talking on the phone, he's a much less
warm version of himself. Actually, he's a little boring and
even kind of cold. But I know he likes me — after all,
alcohol is kind of a truth serum. It helps Matt loosen up,
be himself, and express his feelings. So what do I do? I
obviously don't want him to become a drunk, but I also
want us to feel close.*

What a great pair you make: Matt needs alcohol to feel
comfortable and you're a crack smoker.

Alcohol is not a truth serum. It's a narcotic that impairs
judgment, often leading people to behave in a way that
they normally wouldn't. You're right that booze can

help someone like Matt, who is closed, open up, but that doesn't mean that what he says when he's been drinking is "the truth" or that the way he behaves when he's buzzed is the real him.

The true Matt is the not-under-the-influence-Matt. He's Sober Matt, the guy you think is a bit boring and cold. And, unfortunately, you're just not that into him. (Sounds like Matt doesn't value himself that much either. Eek, how completely un-sexy is that?)

New rule — and hopefully this isn't too earth-shattering — if you don't like someone, you probably shouldn't be dating him. Cut Matt loose. This sauce-soaked asshole will be fine. After all, he's got Johnny Walker and Jim Beam to commiserate with.

And the Asshole Meter says:

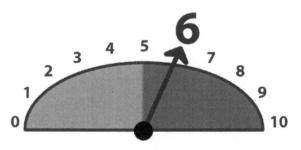

BECAUSE A PERSONALITY MAKEOVER SHOULDN'T COME FROM A BOTTLE

Don't settle for flashes of goodness. Your strongest self knows that any man is only as good as he behaves towards you. If more often than not, he's a great guy who's only usually inconsiderate, he's probably a keeper (no one's perfect!) A good rule of thumb: Look at his intentions. They'll point you to his True North. If, however, he's usually an asshole who's occasionally okay or sometimes awesome, he's your soon-to-be ex. Think of it this way: If three days out of seven with him aren't that fantastic, that's three years out of your next seven and three decades out of the next 70 years. That's half your life. A few moments of greatness seems perfectly fine when dating, but when accumulated over the course of a lifetime, they simply don't add up to happiness, no matter how much you manipulate the math.

****

He Wants a Fuck Buddy, Not a Girlfriend

I met Chris through friends a few weeks ago. He's super hot. We went out on a couple of dates and then started sleeping together. And the sex is GREAT. It's so amazing that we don't even go out. We just stay home and have sex! But then, last week, I randomly bumped into him at a friend's party. I went up to him to say hello and he was really cold, like he was worried I was going to start acting like his girlfriend. Sure, it stung a bit, but I realized immediately what was going on: He's not trying to date me, he's just in it for the sex. But that's totally fine because it's fantastic and I don't want to lose it either. Can't we just use each other?

We're all for sex, even *just* sex. And with a hot guy? Sign us up. Unless, by *just* sex, you mean the kind of arrangement that doesn't include mutual respect.

You're not admitting it, but Chris made you feel cheap. That's how women feel when a man they're burning bed calories with doesn't treat them with common courtesy. And a guy who doesn't get that is an asshole. The second Chris was straight up rude to you in front of other people — behavior we like to describe as a Public Display of Asshole or *PDA* — it should have been game over. Time to take your marbles and go home, no matter how open-minded or progressive you think you are (or how raging your hormones).

We applaud the spirit behind your "If he can do it, I can do it" attitude. But, if you try to compete with a man when it comes to emotionally detaching from sex, you will undoubtedly lose. Trust us on this.

Women, for the most part, desire intimacy with someone they're having a sexual relationship with. It's pretty rare that a woman is satisfied with repeated *just* sex with a guy, no matter how hot, even if the guy is kind and respectful. In general, a woman, like you, who is having *just* sex is *just* settling because the guy won't give her more, and it's *just* a little sad.

And the Asshole Meter says:

BECAUSE PDAs REVEAL SOMEONE'S TRUE NATURE

Don't pretend sex doesn't matter. If you like a guy, there will be an emotional component to having sex with him, no matter how hard you pretend there isn't. And if he isn't emotionally engaging with you in the same way, you'll feel a little empty afterwards, at best, and possibly a little cheap. That's just the truth and you should never convince yourself otherwise.

Delay gratification. Your strongest self waits several dates before having sex with a guy she thinks might be boyfriend material. She's honest with herself that, because she likes this guy, the sex would only be satisfying if she felt secure that he was with her for *her* and not just the sex. Rather than risk her feelings or jeopardize a potential relationship with him by giving up the goods too soon, she exercises self-control. Once the guy has demonstrated that he's genuinely interested in her, she'll consider sleeping with him. And your strongest self never worries that a guy might lose interest unless she goes to bed with him — she knows that if a guy likes her for the right reasons and is actually looking for a relationship, his interest in her will only increase the longer that she doesn't give it up. If his interest diminishes, then she dodged a bullet.

CHAPTER THREE

The Guy Who's Conflicted About You

He Believes You Have a Shelf Life

I met Kevin, who's 42, last year when I was 37 and we started dating. Things have been getting serious and the topic of marriage has come up several times. One night, after the "m" word popped up again, he said, "If I can be honest, I'm struggling with the age thing." Basically, he said that, if it weren't for my age, which concerns him because he wants children, he would have already proposed. I was hurt, but glad we could discuss the situation openly. But as he continued talking, I realized he was breaking up with me. I almost couldn't believe it. Now I'm really hurt and scared. After all, I'm 38 and, if I haven't found a guy yet, maybe I never will.

Women don't have an expiration date. Any man that makes you feel like you do is an asshole. Period.

Kevin doesn't earn this dishonor because he wants to date a younger woman. What makes him lame is that he's rejecting you – a woman he says he would otherwise propose to – on the basis of something that is completely out of your control. That's weak. A stronger man would see past your age (which is so not a big deal, by the way) and gear up for a lifetime with you, the woman he loves, no matter what comes.

What Kevin doesn't understand is that there are no guarantees in life. It's unpredictable on a moment-by-moment basis. Women in their 40s get pregnant all the time — without medical intervention or divine acts of God — and 20- and 30-somethings unfortunately sometimes can't. It's a genetic toss of the dice and you never know what you're gonna roll.

When it comes to finding a partner, Kevin's goal, like yours, should be to find the person with whom he'll most enjoy the good things, whatever they turn out to be, and best get through the bad, whatever those may be. If that was you for Kevin, then he missed out. But don't worry, this lesson will smack Kevin straight in the, er, ego, when his 22-year- old girlfriend asks him what those little blue pills are.

And the Asshole Meter says:

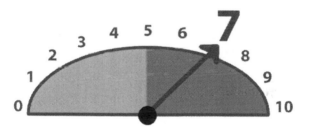

BECAUSE YOU SHOULD MATTER MORE THAN YOUR AGE

Remember, you're the objective. Your strongest self doesn't want a man whose endgame isn't her. She knows there are men out there who always wanted biological children *until* they fell in love with a woman who couldn't fulfill that need — and they accepted that reality because marrying their wife was their ultimate goal. *She* was the prize they wanted, above all else. Your strongest self trusts that man exists for her, someone who will stand beside her as they do their best to have children (if that's what they decide they want) and, if they can't, turn to one of the many alternatives, *together*. It's normal to feel the pressure of a tick-tocking biological clock and worry the odds are shifting against you. But your strongest self knows that this kind of thinking is just self-sabotage. It's unhealthy and unproductive. Instead, she reminds herself that just because something hasn't happened yet, doesn't mean it's not just about to happen. So she looks forward to the future, excited to meet her guy at any moment.

Don't waste your youth thinking you're old.

Thirty-eight feels old … until you turn 39 and suddenly 38 looks pretty damn good. And you might hate being 45 when you're 45, but you'll miss it terribly when you're 50. So do yourself a favor and appreciate the present as though you're an 80 year old who's been given a chance to come back and live a day in your mighty-fine 38-year-old body. Take a moment to let that sink in … see how good it feels! Your strongest self has figured out that perspective is everything. She appreciates the abundance in her life today and moves through her world like she's lucky and blessed *now*. Later, when she rocks her 100th birthday and looks back over the years, she'll have zero regrets.

****

He Wants a Skinny Bitch

Jack and I have been together for two years and I'm pretty sure we'll end up together — he brings up marriage more than I do. The only thing that stresses me out are his extreme views about weight. He told me that he absolutely can't be in love with someone who's overweight. Of course, he knows that I would gain weight when I got pregnant but he's half-joked that I would just have to lose the pounds really fast. This kind of attitude scares me a little. That said, I'm in great shape now and intend to always be healthy. Should I write this off as one of his weird little quirks?

Your partner's irrational fear of a little fat is really just masking his own insecurities and his inability to love you unconditionally. That does not make him quirky. It makes him an asshole.

It's wonderful that you're in shape now, but you have no way of guaranteeing your ass will stay high and tight, even if you dedicate your life to lunges and squats. And once you have kids, you'll be surprised how quickly a toned tush takes a backseat to changing diapers and slinging baby food. And if Jack's wish list remains the same — a thin wife at all costs — you're going to end up not just resenting him, but also feeling pretty shitty about yourself. No man, not even Six-Pack Jack, is worth that.

Any guy who shamelessly declares that he can't love, be attracted to, or respect someone because of a physical attribute — and especially one as common as having a little extra junk in your trunk — is fundamentally flawed. Sorry, but no matter how ripped Jack is, he's not attractive. Kick this fat-phobe to the curb.

And the Asshole Meter says:

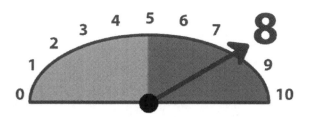

BECAUSE YOU'RE NOT YOUR APPEARANCE

Banish insecurity from your life. Insecurity is one of the most useless emotions. Think about it: What has it done for you lately? Not a goddamn thing right? Except maybe keep you down. That's why you need to do everything in your power not to indulge the voice of your weakest self. Anytime you question whether you're skinny enough, or pretty enough, or funny enough, or charming enough, recognize that those thoughts are among the least productive, most self-defeating thoughts you'll ever have in your lifetime. They serve no positive purpose. In fact, they're dangerous, because they shift focus from the beauty of who you are to some sad imagined version of you that's a figment of your weaker self's fears. The only inner voice worth listening to is that of your strongest self. She'll remind you of your gifts and keep you focused on your world of possibilities. Her support will be among the most important and empowering guidance you'll receive in your lifetime: You are what you believe, and you get what you expect, so by following her affirmations, you can and will achieve anything. No matter what some asshole says.

Rock what yo mama gave you. You know how some women who aren't conventionally pretty are really hot? It's because they know how to work whatever they were born with. Sometimes it's in the way they dress — they know what works for whatever body they have. Sometimes it's in the way they do their hair or makeup — amazing what a blow out and some mascara can do. But there's *always* something special about their attitude. They exude confidence. And that's by far the sexiest attribute you can have. In fact, any woman can dramatically increase her hotness factor within seconds by doing nothing other than acting like she's comfortable with herself. Try it. Sometime, when you're walking down the street, imagine that you look like a Victoria's Secret model. Pretend that you magically have that kind of face and body. Without even trying, you'll feel your walk change, because when a woman feels sexy, she walks a little differently, with her shoulders back and her hips more pronounced. You'll also notice that you suddenly want to hold your head higher than normal and raise your eyebrows a bit, widening your eyes. As you continue down the street, you'll see that more people are making eye contact with you or smiling at you. That's because when you act like you're sexy, people think you're sexy. Remember that every time you walk into a room, especially if you're having a bad hair day, have a big zit, or feel bloated. Don't slouch or wilt or hide behind your hair ... be your strongest self. Act like you're a 10 and all anyone will see is the independence and self-assurance you're radiating.

****

He's Team Jesus. You're Team Buddha.

PJ and I are talking a lot about getting engaged, which has brought up our spiritual beliefs. We're from different backgrounds and neither of us grew up religiously or has practiced as an adult. But since marriage has come up, PJ's parents have been pressuring him to make sure the kids are raised according to their doctrines. I agreed to honor their wishes, because I think all religions are basically the same. Now he's also wondering if he's making the right decision to marry outside of his faith. I'm shocked and not sure what to do.

PJ's not an asshole for caring so much about religion. He's an asshole for *suddenly* caring so much about it.

When one major issue, like religion, ethnicity, or race, keeps a couple from going to the altar, it's usually because they never thought to discuss the issue earlier or because one or both of their viewpoints flip-flopped once the prospect of marriage became real.

That's not acceptable.

If an issue matters to your guy so much that he can't get hitched without it, he should've been straightforward from the beginning. If he didn't realize it mattered to him until after things started getting serious, then it must not have been that important and he should be willing to compromise.

And that's what we think is going on with PJ. He doesn't really know what matters to him. So, when his parents tried to pressure him into marrying someone of his own religion, he thought, "Yes! That is what I need!" even though that didn't occur to him before. And we'd bet that if you sat him down and tried to convince him otherwise, there's a good chance he'd walk away thinking, "Yeah! She's right! I love her and it doesn't matter what her religion is."

But the bigger point is why should you try to convince PJ of anything? If he can't figure this one out on his own, he's just an asshole.

And the Asshole Meter says:

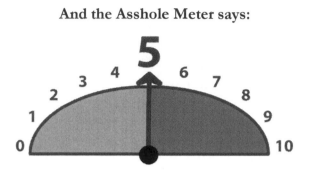

BECAUSE YOU SHOULD KNOW WHAT YOU WANT

Know your deal breakers. People often forget to ask important questions when they're in a relationship: Do you both want to have kids? How will you raise them? Will you both always work? Where will you live? What role will religion play? You may not want to rock the boat by poking around too much too soon, but your strongest self knows that it's the smartest way to making both of you happy. After all, you don't want to just *end up* with someone — you want a true partner based on shared values, principles, and priorities. And you don't want to end up without someone either, which is what could happen in between picking out a wedding venue and a wedding dress, if you don't ask the obvious questions.

CHAPTER FOUR

The Guy Who's Just Not Ready to Commit

He Wants to Test-Drive You For a While First

Justin and I have been dating for three months. We see each other several times a week, have fun together and treat each other well. He's basically my boyfriend and I'm basically his girlfriend. That said, we never use those words and it feels a little funny. I brought it up with him a few days ago. It turns out that this is something he's really thought about. He told me that he has a six-month rule — he said that he takes commitment really seriously so he thinks it makes sense for two people to spend six months "seeing each other" before deciding to be in a relationship. I was disappointed, but at the same time, is that really such a bad thing?

We think you should tell Justin that you have a strict No Assholes policy. And, sadly, because he is one, he's gotta go.

Justin's rule was not decreed by God or the state. It was decreed by Justin. And that means he can break it whenever he wants without having to go to hell or jail. That's a nice situation for the all-powerful Justin. Naturally, he would break this steadfast policy in a flash for a girl that he was really into. And that means that he's just not that into you. Sorry. Even worse, he's hiding this small detail so he can get some companionship out of you until the right girl comes along. After all, he does like you, just not in the way you deserve.

And that's why he's landed such a high asshole rating — he's trying to trick you into sticking around.

Think about it. What if, when you asked him about your status as a couple, he told you that he just didn't dig you enough to commit to you yet. What would you have done? Chances are, walked away (please tell us you would've walked away ...). But Justin is shrewd. He calculated this whole rule thing — a lie, and a lame one at that — to keep you around without having to owe you anything. What's worse is that you're almost buying it!

The reason Justin didn't nail a complete "10" on the Asshole Meter is because he's not a *total* lying sack of shit. See, there's a reason Justin was clear with you that he's not willing to be your "boyfriend." It's because that label creates expectations in you and obligations for him. If Justin was your boyfriend, you would expect him to do certain boyfriendy things (like not bed other women) and he would feel obligated to do certain boyfriendy things (like not bed other women). Justin is unwilling to do those things (like not bed other women) so he fabricated this rule bullshit to manage your expectations rather than completely lead you on. Awwww, that's almost sweet.

Dump him and free yourself from wondering what he's doing during the nights he's not with you. (Though, really, how much mental gymnastics are required to figure that one out?)

And the Asshole Meter says:

BECAUSE HE DOESN'T GET TO TEST-DRIVE YOU FOR MONTHS

Put it through the sniff test. If it smells like bullshit, it probably is. Bad guys are masters at making bad excuses — "I got locked out, I had to sleep at her place" or "no baby, that vibrating G-string belongs to my sister" — and, while a girl shouldn't be paranoid, she should stay on her toes. Your strongest self strikes a great balance between maintaining a healthy skepticism when she's getting to know someone and not buying into a situation that reeks of deception.

Walk if it's not developing organically. Your strongest self knows that the best relationships grow naturally and authentically. Two people meet, there's a spark, they spend time together, and the bond deepens into a relationship. If, after spending time with a guy, things don't seem to be progressing, your strongest self doesn't sit him down and ask him to explain to her what's happening. She can read the tea leaves. Instead, she sits him down and *explains to him* that, by this point, she'd hoped they would have felt closer, but because something clearly isn't working, it makes sense to move on. Next time you're in this situation, channel her mojo. If your guy is truly Mr. Right, he'll fight for you. If he says something real and compelling, not just some nice-sounding clichés, give him a second chance. If not, let him go and move one step closer to finding a true connection with someone willing to invest in you.

****

He's Not Ready to Retire His Bachelor Status

Mark and I have been dating for four years. We're both 34 and, while I'm starting to get antsy about marriage, he's not ready to settle down. I have no doubt that we'll end up together, but the waiting game is frustrating. I don't understand. Just last night, the topic came up again and I asked him why he's dragging his feet. His response: "I'm waiting to be ready." I almost ripped his head off. He's such a great guy and I know it's normal for men to be scared. And so many of them end up marrying the woman they kept waiting anyway. How much time does he need?

Ding! Time's up, Mark.

Ya know all those men who married the women they kept on hold? Those men married their back-up plans. Unfortunately that's what you become when a guy refuses to tie the knot for no good reason, for way too long. Four years? That's an entire presidential term or a stint in undergrad. Does Mark need the same amount of time to determine whether you're right for him? We think not.

Of all those lucky ladies who finally, after waiting and waiting, landed "The One", we bet a whole lot of them would've found a guy for whom they weren't just a back-up plan, if only they weren't trapped in a no-win situation, exhausting their patience and self-worth.

Yes, it's difficult to leave a comfortable relationship, even if it's one-sided and unhealthy, because it looks a lot better than the alternative — being alone. The irony is that more often than not, as soon as a woman walks away from what's not serving her, the asshole who treated her like a backup plan suddenly turns into a prince who realizes she's The One. And for others, their fairytale begins when they walk out the door and into the arms of a new man. Either way, the woman who walks wins.

We say, roll the dice and see what happens. What's a girl got to lose? Just one asshole? That sounds like a lot less baggage.

And the Asshole Meter says:

BECAUSE IF HE DOESN'T KNOW HE WANTS YOU, HE SHOULD LET YOU GO

Walk if you want to win. When a guy says he needs more time, your first inclination may be to give in and sit there, like a puppy, waiting to follow his lead. The fear of being alone is greater than the fear of losing yourself. How scary, and sad, is that? The reality is that you'll never find someone wonderful while you're wasting your time on some guy who's not ready to be fully present in your life. Your strongest self knows this. She never waits. If a guy needs time, she bounces. If he wants to be with her, he'll prove that through his actions, not his sweet talk. And that's how it should be because you have better places to be, things to do, guys to meet.

Play like you have a weak hand and you'll lose, every time. The biggest difference between people who have more and those who have less is that the ones who have more believe they deserve it.

Because what you expect is a self-fulfilling prophecy. Accept less, become less, get less. Expect more, become more, get more. So never take less than you deserve, betraying a weak hand. Even when you're feeling weak — especially when you're feeling weak, in fact — *bluff*. Always play like you're holding a royal flush. Always. And you might just win the jackpot.

****

He's Stuck in a Professional Rut

A coworker introduced me to Hugh about a year ago. We have a great relationship in every respect except we only see each other a couple of times a week. The problem is he's in a rut professionally. He got laid off a few years ago and had to take a job that doesn't pay well. He says that he can't fully focus on a relationship until he gets back on track. When I complain, which is rarely, he reminds me that he cares deeply for me, isn't seeing anyone else, and wants to get to a place where he can buy me dinner (we often go dutch). He swears that once he's not distracted by his work situation, he'll be able to spend a lot more time with me — you know, really act like my boyfriend. My friends tell me Hugh's just not that into me, but I think he loves me and is just going through a rough patch. What do you think?

It's possible that Hugh's just not that into you. But frankly we don't care. Because we're certain he's an asshole. And that's pretty much all that matters. Hugh is not *incapable* of giving you more right now, he's simply decided not to. That's a major distinction. If he were a good guy, he'd push himself to do the right thing and work harder to fulfill your needs since you're working so hard to fulfill his. But he's not a good guy. He's selfish and lazy.

But there's more: Hugh's also an idiot. While he's sulking over not being able to afford to take you out, he's overlooking the beautiful reality staring him in the face — he's found a girl who loves him even though he's not bankrolling her diamonds and dinners!

But wait. Let's pretend for a moment that Hugh has just been offered his dream job and is about to transform into the man you have been fantasizing about all this time.

Woo-hoo! Yippee! Yay!

Right?

Wrong.

Do you really want a guy who can treat you well only when it's easy or convenient? Someone who's shown his predisposition to collapse and put everything on hold when the going gets tough? Even if your answer to that is yes — if so, now would be a good time to pause and reflect on that — it's never going to come to that, thank God.

Because Hugh will, in fact, change once he gets a new job. He'll dump you and change who he's dating.

When Hugh's luck turns, if ever, he's going to feel like a big swinging dick and will run to the rooftops shouting out his new and improved status, beating his chest. Hanging out with you — the once-attractive woman who became less and less so thanks to Hugh being a taker and not a giver —— is not going to be his idea of a good time. He'll want to be with the sexy, carefree girl who values herself so highly that she would never put up with the crap Hugh's been dishing you. What'll you have to show for standing by your man through his dark days? Nada, my friend.

And no big surprise, that makes Hugh an asshole.

And the Asshole Meter says:

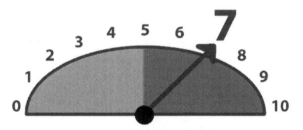

BECAUSE A HEAD CASE NEEDS A GOOD SHRINK, NOT A GOOD WOMAN

Steer clear of self-proclaimed losers. People who feel sorry for themselves and think their lives are worse than they actually are self-pitying pessimists who can't see outside their own bubble. If a guy doesn't value himself, he certainly won't value the woman who's willing to hang around with him. Your strongest self knows that. So, when a man tells her he can't commit until he's in a better place, she believes him, and suggests he calls her when he gets there. Or not.

Don't get sucked into the vortex of someone else's misery. Negativity and hopelessness can be contagious if you're around them too much. It's commendable to help someone through a difficult period but unless you're in a serious and deeply committed relationship, don't date them through it. When you're with someone who's depressed or down, the priorities of the relationship often shift to mood management and caretaking. Your role moves from partner to pseudo-therapist, mom, and emotional punching bag. And once they're better, the relationship might be worse for the wear. Your strongest self is compassionate and wants to help those in need but she also recognizes that it's sometimes best to play that part from a greater distance, as a friend.

Don't go dutch. We're not saying that the guy should always pay. But we do know that, in general, when a guy really likes a girl, he wants to pay and will likely insist upon it. It makes him feel like a stud. If the guy you're with isn't trying to pay – and you suspect he could afford to – he's either cheap or doesn't have right intentions. After all, springing for dates is a gesture of romance and respect and you deserve both of those things.

****

He's Too Busy to Get Hitched

My fiancé Michael has the job from hell. He's a junior partner at a big law firm and he's insanely busy, all the time. We started dating four years ago when he was still an associate and we barely saw each other. He assured me that his life would improve once he made partner, but it's almost worse! Most days, we only see each other for a few minutes really late at night or early in the morning. When he is free, we'll be really low-key because he's so tired. He says it'll get better when he's no longer a "junior" partner, but I just don't know. I'm 33 and want to get married and start a family. But he's very clear that he can't even begin to imagine planning a wedding for a while given his crazy schedule. I do love him and have no doubt that we're going to spend our lives together. It's just a question of when we'll tie the knot and how much I'll get to see this man who I love so much. Any words of wisdom?

Working sucks. But, sadly, we can't all go around quitting our jobs willy nilly. It's complicated. We get that.

What we don't get is why Michael doesn't do a better job of balancing work and his relationship. There are many highly successful people in the world, after all, who have insanely busy careers, yet manage to have healthy personal lives that don't leave their partners feeling neglected. We've actually seen these people with our own eyes — we know they exist.

The cold, harsh reality: Michael is a rock star on the job,

but a lazy bastard in your relationship.

There are a million little things Michael could do with minimal effort that would make you feel more attended to, but he consciously *chooses* not to do them. He (or his assistant) could make a reservation for a romantic dinner a couple of times a month. He's got to eat, right? Or he could make you breakfast in bed every once in a while. Or send you quick little notes via e-mail or text a few times a week, even something as simple as, "Miss you. Sorry I'm working late." If he types 60 words a minute, that text will take 10 seconds to write. And the list of possibilities goes on.

But Michael decides to do nothing. And he actively makes that choice every day, in large part, because you let him. He takes you for granted. He knows you'll be there, taking what little he's offering. In fact, he's come to expect it.

We think you should have some expectations too, such as a life that is not spent waiting for someone, aka an asshole, who doesn't understand the importance of balance or the value of a partner who loves and supports you, aka an asshole.

And the Asshole Meter says:

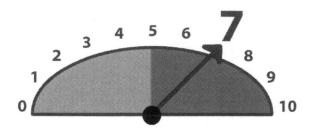

BECAUSE IT'S THE LITTLE THINGS THAT SPEAK THE LOUDEST

Notice his choices. People make thousands, if not millions, of decisions every day. Everything we do — the route we take to work, where we eat for lunch, what we say or don't say in any given moment — is a deliberate choice. And your strongest self knows that men make choices every day about how to interact with their girlfriends. When a guy says he was too busy to call, she knows that he probably could have called or sent a note, but chose not to. And that's sometimes okay — because your strongest self isn't unreasonable or needy. But she's also not afraid to acknowledge a bad pattern of behavior when she sees it. If her guy always blames his shitty decision making on factors beyond his control, she knows what's going on: Either she's not a priority or he's really bad at balancing his life. And while neither of those is acceptable, she has a starting point for initiating a conversation or packing a suitcase.

Keep your life full. When a woman likes a guy, she often makes him the focal point of her life thinking that, the more she gives, the more she'll get in return.

Sadly, it doesn't work that way. Generally speaking, a man's interest in satisfying a woman's needs rises in relation to how much independence she continues to maintain. That's because people value the things that are scarce the most. The harder something is to find — like a beautiful diamond — the more people are willing to pay for it. Similarly, the more full a woman's life and the busier she is attending to her own needs, the more a man will desire her, and the more he will appreciate the time he spends with her. Your strongest self understands this. That doesn't mean she runs around playing hard to get just so a man will want her. She doesn't do anything just to land a man. Rather, she prioritizes her own needs as an expression of her self-respect and self-worth. No matter how in love she is, she continues being social by spending time with her girlfriends and cultivating other friendships. She enjoys her time on her own and expanding her knowledge. She pursues her own interests and loves trying new things. Your most important pursuit is ensuring your own health and happiness, which in turn creates greater health and happiness for those you love.

****

He's Nursing a Broken Heart

Thomas and I started dating a few months after his engagement to his girlfriend ended. (Apparently, she cheated on him with a friend and the whole thing was ugly and traumatic.) When we met, he wasn't looking for a relationship, but we hit it off and we've been dating for a few weeks. Things are mostly good, except that he holds back sometimes. Like he doesn't want to get too close. I asked him about it and he said he needs a little space for a few months — which I totally understand after what he went through — and he asked if we could just keep things as they are. I don't mind that because we do see each other a lot ... I just want to make sure that we're on our way to a full relationship.

We'd feel really bad for poor, broken-hearted Thomas if it wasn't for the fact that he's about to stomp on your heart. And we like you more, because you're not an asshole, you're just gullible.

Let's back up.

If you had just been dumped and were left with a broken heart and then, a few months later, your dream guy — say, Leo DiCaprio or Channing Tatum — wanted to date you, would you tell them you just need to take it slow? Or would you do everything you could to look hot, be fun, and open yourself to the possibility of this exciting new relationship?

That was a rhetorical question.

Don't shoot the messenger, but you're not Thomas's dream girl. If you were, he'd be over his broken heart, jumping through hoops to date you. Instead, he's trying to keep things simple. He wants to enjoy your company until he finds the girl he really wants to date. Instead of being honest about that fact, this guy you feel so bad for is going to string you along like a little kitten.

And the Asshole Meter says:

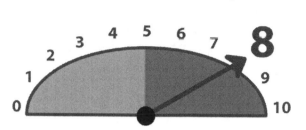

BECAUSE "TAKING IT SLOW" IS CODE FOR "BUYING TIME"

When a guy tells you who he is, listen. Especially when it's not complimentary. When a man says "I'm not ready for anything serious" or "I'm bad at relationships", pay attention. He just told you exactly what you can and can't expect from him. When you rationalize for a guy or create stories on his behalf, you convince yourself to go against his truth. Usually at your own peril. He told you up front the kind of man he is and what he's willing to give. So the ball is in your court — we say, take it and go home. If you choose to stay in an unhealthy situation, you have no one to blame but yourself.

CHAPTER FIVE

The Guy Who's Not Trustworthy

He's Prince Charming

My boyfriend, Daniel, is really charismatic and charming. He can strike up a conversation with anyone. And he often does … with waitresses, shop girls, bartenders, flight attendants. I know he isn't actually hitting on them — I'm right there! — but it's embarrassing. I've told him I don't like it, but he says he's just social. And then he always points out that I'm the only girl he loves and that he's never given me any reason to think he'll stray. He's not wrong — I really have no reason to doubt him. So maybe I should just let this go and accept that this is who he is?

Daniel does sound charming. In fact, he's oozing with so much charm that he can't turn it off, not even for a second! Even when it's demeaning and humiliating to the woman he loves! Now, *that's* charming!

Personally, we think this Prince Charming is a Royal Asshole.

See, Daniel is not just a wildly sociable, overtly friendly, and unacceptably approachable guy. He's also a narcissist. He adores himself. We bet Daniel would make passionate love to himself if he could.

Daniel flirts with everything because it turns him on. He thrives on the sexual tension, the sense of power he feels when he has an effect on a woman, and if he's cheating on you, he's addicted to the excitement of being with someone different or forbidden. He's a thrill seeker who isn't satisfied building and deepening a relationship. Instead, he relishes the rush of newness. Otherwise, poor Daniel gets bored. *That's* why he engages with strangers.

You say your beloved boyfriend has never given you a reason to doubt him. Um, seriously? We'll help you tally up the strikes:

<u>Strike 1</u>: He flirts with random women (and presumably your friends, too)

<u>Strike 2</u>: Shamelessly does it in front of you, suggesting that he thinks it's acceptable

<u>Strike 3</u>: Refuses to curb his behavior even after you've asked him to do so

<u>Strike 4</u>: Consciously subjects you to embarrassment and makes a fool out of you when he drools over another woman in front of you

<u>Strike 5</u>: Repeatedly undermines your relationship every time he hits on someone behind your back.

To be clear: Daniel is more than a man-whore. He's a walking ego trip who has poor judgment and a completely flawed sense of what's appropriate. Sooner or later — and the time bomb is ticking — he's going to woo himself into another woman's bed.

And the Asshole Meter says:

BECAUSE A REAL PRINCE ONLY HAS ONE CINDERELLA

Know your worth. When you're with your guy, he should be focused on you. Not on the waitress. Not on the hottie at the next table. Not on the woman who just strutted past. Sure, we all appreciate eye candy. Stealing a glance here and there is normal, but there's a stark difference between a guy who occasionally notices a fine piece of ass and one who needs a drool cup every time he's in public. Your strongest self is secure enough not to be threatened by the former *and* confident enough to walk away from the latter.

Look at his actions, not his excuses. Intentions are irrelevant when it comes to inappropriate behavior. If you're sticking around a bad guy because "he doesn't mean anything by it" or "that's just how he is", you're letting your weak self drive. Your strongest self knows that a guy doesn't have to intend to hurt you in order to do damage. Causing you pain might just be a consequence of something he enjoys doing, such as flirting or cheating, with other women. He doesn't act this way **to** hurt you, but he does so *even though* it hurts you, and that's all that matters. On the flip side, your strongest self understands that the best relationships are the ones in which each person works at making the other one happy. Having a partner who actively cultivates your happiness is priceless, and you shouldn't settle for anything less.

****

He's a Late Night Texter

I met Alan a few weeks ago. We've gone out a few times and things seem to be moving in the right direction. He does this weird thing sometimes, though — he texts me when he's out to ask if I want to meet up and when I reply, he takes forever to get back to me. Like last night. I was out with some friends when Alan texted me at midnight to join him downtown. I replied sure and asked him where he was and … silence. After an hour, I went home just as he replied with the bar's address. When I told him it was too late, he seemed genuinely bummed out, so I let him come over and we had a great time. When I asked him what took him so long to reply, he said he just got caught up and didn't realize. Maybe he's just one of those people who loses track of time?

When Alan texts you asking you to meet him, you picture him standing there, bored at some bar with a couple of dude friends, fantasizing about how much more fun it would be if you were there. "Aaaw, he misses me," you think as your heart lights up and smiles.

Asshole alert! What's really happening is one of the following:

Worst-case scenario: Alan and his pals are at a packed bar, buying rounds of shots for themselves and a bunch of hot women. They've been chatting up these chicks for a while, but Alan isn't sure that he can close a deal by last call. He's tequila-soaked and wants to make sure the night ends well (read: with a monster orgasm), so he grabs his iPhone and bangs out, "Where are you? Am downtown. Want to meet up?" A couple of clicks later, he blasts that note to you and about 10 other potential love vessels to see who bites.

Next-to-worst-case scenario: Alan thinks it would be fantastic to see you and texts you to meet him. A few minutes later, he starts talking to some babe who brushed up against his zipper on the way to the loo. He forgets you exist.

Best-case scenario: Alan would totally dig seeing you and texts you to meet him. He then puts his phone away and forgets all about you for an hour. Duh.

In any of the above scenarios, Alan is just an asshole. Not only is he incapable of making plans with you in advance, but he can't even commit to plans *as* he's in the middle of making them! That takes talent.

And the Asshole Meter says:

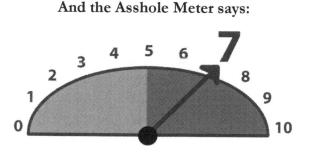

BECAUSE YOU'RE NOT THE LAST CALL AT THE BAR

Refuse to be an afterthought. There are a lot of guys who, toward the end of the night, will text a girl they're getting to know to come meet them at the [insert random bar here]. She often obliges, thinking, "It's no big deal. I'm out, he's out. It would be fun to see him." Naturally, a part of her wishes he'd get off his dead keester to travel to her, but she looks the other way. Hey, at least he wants to see her and it's an opportunity to further their connection. Your strongest self knows this is a steaming crock of bullshit. She's simply not drawn to a guy who treats her like a Plan B. She knows that if he really wanted to see her that night, he would've planned an evening with her in advance. And if he were busy, he would've suggested they try to meet afterward. Texting her out of the blue as his night is winding down? Not hot. In those situations, missing an opportunity with the guy is more like dodging a bullet. We say buy yourself a fresh pack of batteries and call it a night. (Might we add that it's no surprise why a guy like this has no takers when the bartender yells last call?)

Don't reward bad behavior If a deadbeat blows you off, don't reward him with a roll beneath your sheets. We shouldn't have to explain this, but we will. While there are a lot of Grade A guys out there, there are plenty of assholes, too. These predators sniff around for signs that you're easy prey. Their radar goes off if you're weak, insecure or gullible, i.e. if you're willing to compromise yourself. One of the fastest ways to show your hand is to quickly forgive someone who doesn't deserve a break. He calls, you jump to primp and preen, he makes a mental note: "This one's a piece of cake." Your strongest self gets this guy's M.O. and doesn't bite when he dangles the bait. Setting firm boundaries allows you to attract the kind of man you want and deserve to be with. Losers need not apply.

****

He's a Chronic Cheater

Drew and I are dating each other for the second time. The first time we dated, we broke up after two years because he cheated on me a bunch of times. He was 30 then. He's now 34 and we ran into each other at a party recently and drunkenly hooked up. Things are better this time — he seems to have matured a lot. There have been a couple of times, though, when he's freaked me out by not calling me back until the following morning. Each time I asked him what happened, he got upset and warned me that the relationship won't work if I keep putting him under a microscope. Maybe I'm being paranoid and need to trust him?

We're not Drew's mom. That means we don't have to love him unconditionally.

This just in: You're not Drew's mom either.

Next time he gives you his *you're-so-lucky-I'm-giving-you-a-second-chance-so-you-better-shut-up-or-I-might-leave-you-again* attitude, let him in on your own big secret: He's just an asshole. And as he's walking out the door, tell him to go to hell.

Cheaters are among the lowest of the asshole life forms. They're thieves who steal your time and attention under completely false pretenses. You eventually find out your entire relationship was just an illusion and you're left feeling foolish and afraid to trust again.

But, you're not certain that Drew is cheating this time. Even though he gets defensive and accusatory when you ask him where he's been. Hmmm ... Suuure, it's quite possible he's changed. (Did we mention that we have some spectacular oceanfront property in Kansas we'd like to sell you?)

There's no way that the flawed ethical and emotional framework that led Drew to cheat in the first place has been miraculously remodeled. What was his incentive to change? Nada. Unless he's a recent grad of Assholes Anon, we're betting he's still the same lowly bedhopper — the one who believes it's okay to lie to someone when it's convenient. If he's not cheating, it's only because he hasn't been tempted. Yet. You know this, which explains why the pit of your stomach aches when you don't hear from him. Fact: Drew has shown you his True North and it points to someone else's boudoir.

Even worse, your soon-to-be double-ex takes sleeping around to a new low by being callous to boot. Any guy with a track record of deception who makes you feel like a paranoid nag when he disappears for hours on end is, quite frankly, evil. We understand that you somehow fell back into lust with him after a drunken night of what-not, but remember: The first time you dated him, you didn't know how it would end. This time, you do.

And the Asshole Meter says:

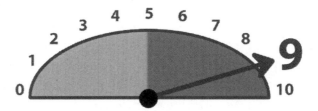

BECAUSE ONCE A LIAR, ALWAYS A LIAR

Don't forgive a cheater. It's really that simple. People who stray have convinced themselves that sneaking around is perfectly acceptable. They mistakenly believe the rules don't apply to them — they're special. And it's almost impossible for someone to live in this altered reality without being, in scientific terms, completely screwed in the head. If a so-called "recovered cheater" hasn't fallen off the wagon, chances are it's because he's not being tempted *right now*. A man who, at a deep level, feels he can do whatever the hell he wants will have zero problem breaking his commitment to you when an enticing opportunity presents itself. It's only a matter of time.

Follow your gut when something feels off. When your intuition nudges you, listen. Because that voice is just your strongest self, whispering in your ear. If her instincts feel something in your relationship isn't right, she sends a warning and you shouldn't just dismiss it. Talk to your guy — if he tells you that you're insane or paranoid, making you second-guess yourself, honestly reflect on who he is. Ask yourself: Is this someone who actively works to make me happy? Has he consistently treated me like a priority? Does he appreciate and respect me? If the answer to any of these questions is "no", or even a "meh", to hell with what he says, thinks or does. He hasn't earned the right to have an opinion, let alone be your man.

****

He Takes You to Parties, Not Dates

Phil and I have been together for three months and I've noticed that he really likes to go out, nearly every night. He's really social and knows tons of people so there's always a game to watch at some bar or a party to go to at some club. He invites me along most of the time, but my going out limit is two to three times a week. Beyond that, it's not fun for me. I'd much rather go to dinner with him alone — we've only ever done that three times! I've brought this up, but he doesn't get it. He says that I need to stop being such a party pooper. Should I just suck it up and drag myself out with him more?

You know what would make you a party pooper? If you started joining Phil every time he went out with his buddies. Because you'd be shitting on his parade, the one he can only have when you're not there.

We have no clue if Phil is cheating, nor do we care. Frankly, it's common sense that part of what draws Phil to da club is da ladies. After all, there's no such thing as a straight dude who hits the party circuit without hunting for chicks. Sorry, doesn't happen.

But even if Phil isn't what we suspect (a two-timing asshole), he still has a problem: He's about as interesting as a pebble. Any guy who spends all his free time in loud places where conversation is limited to small talk and fist pumps is probably also just a shallow loser with nothing interesting to say.

And the Asshole Meter says:

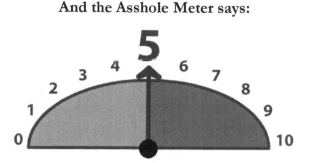

BECAUSE IT'S TOUGH TO BUILD A LASTING RELATIONSHIP IN A MOSH PIT

Expect intimacy. One of the best parts of being in a relationship is the physical and emotional closeness that builds over time, by sharing experiences together, both in groups and one on one. Your strongest self wants a partner she feels close to and can create a real bond with. She knows that without a real connection, she'll feel lonely and unsatisfied. So if her guy would rather go out and talk about the weather with some strangers instead of spending quality time with her, she loses interest in him immediately — and rightfully so. Keep the one-dimensional losers on the dance floor and save the pillow talk for the guys who want to truly know what's on your mind.

Express your preferences. When we like a guy, we often suppress our own desires to make him happy. He wants to see that action flick? Okay. He wants burgers for dinner? Sounds good. He wants to go out tonight instead of stay in? Done. And that's acceptable in a healthy relationship where the willingness to compromise is reciprocal. You watched the dude movie this time, but you know that he'll be willing to watch the tearjerker next time. But in so many relationships, women continually prioritize their guys' needs disproportionately, setting an early precedent that their own wishes aren't important. Your strongest self doesn't do that. Not only is she incapable of not being her authentic self, but also she knows that men don't like malleable women. And she's no pushover. She doesn't stop being herself to please a guy. That doesn't mean she's not agreeable when the situation calls for it; it just means she has opinions and isn't afraid to express them. And that just happens to make her very attractive because the hottest women are the ones who are so secure in their own desirability that they barely notice a guy unless *he's* trying very hard to win *them*.

****

He Overlaps Girlfriends

My boyfriend and I had been together for four months when I found out that he had a girlfriend for the first two months we were dating. I had no idea until I met his ex randomly at a party. And she had no idea he broke up with her for another girl. He just told her they were done and cut her off. I'm surprised that he cheated on her and never told me, but I'm thinking I shouldn't make too big a deal out of it either — after all, he and I weren't technically exclusive at that point even though we were spending a lot of time together. So maybe I shouldn't overthink it?

The critical question is not whether Sean was "technically" cheating on you, it's: How big of an asshole is he?

Answer: Pretty freakin' huge.

Dating is complicated. When you first start spending time with someone, it's tough to know what to expect. You're not yet exclusive and you're both aware that each of you might be seeing other people. But there is one thing that you should be able to expect: That the other person is unattached, and not in a committed relationship.

What if Sean had told you the truth — that he had a girlfriend, wasn't sure if he wanted to stay with her, and was just test-driving you to see if that helped him make up his mind?

We're betting you would have walked away. Not only would you have been skeeved that this guy who was trying to date you was a cheater, but you also probably wouldn't have wanted to get caught up in someone who wasn't fully available.

Sean knew his situation wouldn't fly with any rational woman, so he lied to you. He represented himself as being on an even playing field with you — a swinging single looking for love — when, in fact, he still had one foot in the bedroom door of another relationship.

But, lucky you! It worked out beautifully. After two

months of crashing with both you and his girlfriend, he was *finally* ready to pick. And you were the chosen one [cue the wedding bells]. Congrats! That dreamboat is now all yours ... at least until he decides to diversify his love portfolio again.

And the Asshole Meter says:

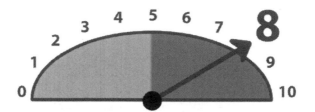

BECAUSE MYSTERY MEN ARE ONLY SEXY IN MOVIES

Look at how his last relationship ended. How he treats others is a telltale sign for how he'll behave with you. If your guy cheated on his ex and dumped her with little to no explanation, that could be your future. Sure, the honeymoon period may still be smooth, but what happens when he gets bored down the road? Your strongest self pays attention to not just how a guy acts with her, but also how he operates with other people in his life: his exes, his friends, his family. She knows that at the core of a person's behavior is his character and that, when the going gets tough, character will determine how respectfully and ethically he reacts.

Steer clear of secret keepers. You and your guy are supposed to share with each other certain important information about your lives, including your pasts. While it's not required — and actually not advisable — to deep-dive into details about earlier romances, you should have some sense of a person's dating history. How many important relationships has he had? How long have they lasted? What led to some of their more significant break ups? If you don't know that your boyfriend's last relationship ended two months into the time yours began, that's a serious red flag. Your guy keeps secrets. Your strongest self realizes that it's not smart to partner with anyone who's not transparent, especially about the important issues. If you do, fast-forward 10 years and you're suddenly starring in the next Lifetime movie about the pilot's wife who had no clue her jetsetting husband had separate families hidden throughout the globe.

****

He Has Endless Phone Excuses

I adore Travis, my boyfriend of the last year, but he has a bad habit. If he's out with his guy friends, he sometimes doesn't answer my calls or texts. A few times, I haven't heard from him for hours or all night. He always has a legitimate-sounding reason: There was no signal in the club, his phone was with his jacket in coat check or it ran out of juice. I'm not a fool — I know that he's sometimes telling little white lies, but I can't figure out if he's lying to hide the fact that he was having fun and didn't want to talk to me, or if he was up to something worse. Part of me thinks I'm being paranoid because if he were a cheater, he'd do a better job of hiding his tracks and just text me, right?

Let's get this straight: You're saying that the more it looks like a guy is hiding something, the less likely he's actually hiding something because, if he were actually hiding something, he'd manage to do it more effectively.

Um, right.

You get an A+ in Denial and an F in Asshole Detection.

There's only one reason Travis habitually doesn't take your calls when he's out: He doesn't want to deal with you. Talking to you detracts from Boys Night Out so, instead, he dishes you every lame excuse in the book. And you buy them.

Why is that asshole behavior? Please review the previous chapters on prioritizing you, showing common courtesy, and acting transparently.

On that note, the likelihood that Travis's fun is limited to standing at a bar, bullshitting with his dude friends is pretty slim. Why wouldn't he hit on a hot girl? After all, he doesn't think you're so wonderful. If he did, he'd take your calls.

And the Asshole Meter says:

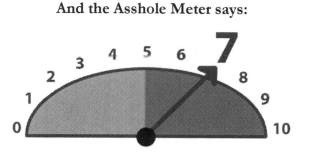

BECAUSE IT'S NOT THAT HARD TO MANAGE YOUR PHONE

Beware of brazen assholes. Don't assume a guy's suspicious behavior is somehow less so because he chooses to do it right in front of you. That just means he's not only an asshole, but a shameless one at that. He feels so entitled to behave the way he wants that he's not even thinking about whether it's acceptable or hurtful. He doesn't care. Your strongest self takes a zero tolerance approach to guys like this. She knows that a man who'll openly flirt with another woman right in front of you wouldn't think twice about doing her in your bed either.

Pay attention to the small lies. A little white lie is generally harmless and well-intentioned — "no, I can't see your muffin top" or "yes, dear, yours is the biggest I've ever seen." But sorry, "I dropped my phone in the toilet" when your guy doesn't want to talk to you doesn't qualify. Even if he isn't a cheating rat bastard, it's still bad because he clearly thinks he has to lie to keep you from getting mad at him. That means he doesn't trust you enough to be honest with you, and that leads to you not being able to trust him. If that's your situation, it might as well end because, as your strongest self knows, a relationship without trust is going nowhere fast.

****

He's Got a Dirty Little Secret: You

I met Keith a couple of months ago at a party. We went back to my place and hooked up — it was really fun! Since then, he's stayed over a few times and gone to a couple of parties with me and my friends. The weird thing is that I've never met any of his friends. I asked him about it, but he said that they're lame. The night I met him, though, he came to the party with a big group of people and they looked pretty interesting. Maybe he just likes what we have going and doesn't want to ruin the dynamic by bringing other people into it?

Let's put on our big girl panties and admit that the only thing that'll get ruined if Keith introduces you to his friends is his game.

When two people start dating, they want to share their worlds with each other. They want to introduce their new partner to their friends, they want to introduce their friends to their new partner. They want to enjoy the social options created when all these worlds overlap.

The only time someone doesn't want their worlds to

collide is when they're trying to hide something. And in most cases, it's the fact that they're cheating. Another explanation is that Keith wants a fuck buddy, not a true relationship, or he wouldn't exclude you from his life. That's fantastic, except for the small, but important, detail that you're under a different impression.

Either way, we spot an asshole.

And the Asshole Meter says:

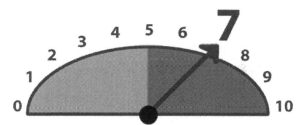

BECAUSE HE DOESN'T WANT YOU IF HE HIDES YOU

Ditch mystery men. While an air of mystery works in a 007 scenario, it's an unfulfilling, deceptive time suck in the real world. Either the guy you date includes you in his life and wants to be a part of yours, or you fast-track to someone who's happy to share his world with you. Whenever a man comes to the table without a certain level of transparency, openness, and emotional availability, it's a red flag. There's a reason he wants to remain a stranger in your life — and it's not likely one that's legit.

CHAPTER SIX

The Guy Who's Insecure

He Needs to be Alpha Dog

My boyfriend, Ken, and I are both lawyers. He was up for partner at his firm two years ago and didn't make it. I felt awful for him because I knew how much he wanted it. A few months ago, I made partner at my firm. I was thrilled, but downplayed my excitement because I didn't want to make him feel bad. He was nice about it — he sent flowers to my office — but other than that, it barely came up. And I'm not gonna lie: I was a little bummed that he didn't do more. And since then, although we talk about his work, he doesn't seem to want to hear about mine. I don't like that he's being weird, but can understand how he feels. Should I just continue to stand by him until he's past this?

There are men who take pride in their partner's accomplishments and see her successes as their own. And then there are the insecure assholes who feel threatened by them. Like Ken.

Making partner is a huge achievement. We're guessing it involved grueling 12-hour days for years on end. That's no joke, and if anyone should empathize with how hard you worked, it's your lawyer boyfriend. He knows how much you struggled for this and how badly you must've wanted it — probably about as much as he did! — and when you landed it, the best he could do was phone

FTD. Hello, 1-800-Asshole? We've got a live one.

Just for a second, imagine if Ken had made partner. What would you have done for him? The celebration probably would've lasted for days and likely involved aphrodisiac-filled dinners, never-ending bottles of champagne, and mindblowing sex acts a girl usually saves for special occasions.

We understand that Ken is dealing with disappointment, but it's not cool to let your insecurities sabotage your partner's success. His happiness for you should trump his own selfish pride. A guy who's more invested in soothing his bruised ego than supporting your big win needs to be left wallowing in his own self-pity. Your man should be on Team You and, if for some reason, he drops out of the race, he should still stand on the sidelines, rooting for you at every mile. If not, we hear the loser's tent is looking for a few men just like him.

And the Asshole Meter says:

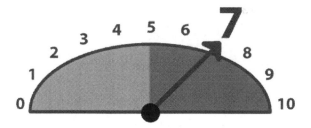

BECAUSE YOUR SUCCESS IS NOT MUTUALLY EXCLUSIVE WITH HIS

Avoid guys with excessive ego. A lot of guys, in order to feel like "real men", need to believe they're more successful than their women. Similarly, many women prefer the security of knowing their men are "taking care of them" financially. That's not awful (as long as you're on the same page) — and some might even argue this thinking is evolutionary. But your strongest self knows that the most important question when it comes to a couple's professional power dynamic is not who the top dog is, but whether you can both survive and thrive whatever shitstorm life throws at you, no matter who's bringing home the bacon. Because the best relationships are about adapting to make it work, whatever happens next. So, if you're lighting the world on fire and he chooses to be consumed by jealousy rather than excited for your success, leave him right where he belongs — alone, at the head table of his own pity party.

Never minimize your accomplishments. Showing off is not sexy. Neither is diminishing yourself to keep a guy who needs you to be small so he feels secure. Your strongest self knows this. She realizes that because she's confident, she needs a rock-solid man, one whose ego is not so fragile that he can't appreciate what an amazing woman she is. The guy she's after knows that the good things in life ebb and flow. While he might have to step aside to let his lady shine today, he'll be in the spotlight next. A true partnership considers each person's success as "theirs", not his or hers.

****

He Hits Below the Belt

My boyfriend James is a sweetheart … when we're getting along. Whenever we get into an argument, though, he doesn't fight fair. For example, I was upset because I thought he was flirting with his ex at a party and when I brought it up, he got overly defensive and pointed out that one of my exes works in my office. When I said that was different, he said that I don't understand logic and called me a stupid idiot who can't even spell (I'm dyslexic). In other fights, he's said that I come from trash, that I suck in bed, that I'm fat. I know he doesn't mean these things because he always apologizes immediately and goes back to normal. Since it's obviously just his anger talking, should I forgive and forget?

How would you feel if your boyfriend was usually nice to you except those couple of times a month when he punched you in the face?

While James doesn't physically batter you, the violent comments he makes during fights are verbally abusive. He's assaulting you with words, slowly chipping away at your sense of self, which is just slightly less horrible than striking you with the back of his hand. And like a textbook abuser, James apologizes profusely right after so you can't stay mad at him. It works brilliantly for him — he causes you pain but suffers no consequence.

On the abuse spectrum, the difference between verbal and physical abuse is just shades of gray — or one really awful, out-of-control fight. And just as anger doesn't excuse physical abuse, it doesn't justify verbal abuse. Healthy people control themselves. They self-regulate. They respect boundaries. They express their emotions and thoughts through love and compassion, not by yelling or hurling insults. In any relationship, it's a normal part of intimacy to know your partner's Achilles Heel, the single most hurtful thing you can say or do that will bring them to their knees. But that's the nuclear option and, because you'd never want to cause James pain, you'd never go there. Meanwhile, James clearly knows your vulnerabilities and doesn't hesitate to go for the jugular.

James isn't healthy. He's weak and he knows it. He's so insecure, in fact, that he acts as though he's being attacked even when he's not. And the feeling of being under siege leads James to lash out at his "attacker", even though she's just his girlfriend, trying to have a normal conversation. Do you really want to stick around to see what happens when he really gets enraged?

We'll answer for you: Leave. James is an abuser. For now, his weapon is words but, eventually, it will be his fist.

And the Asshole Meter says:

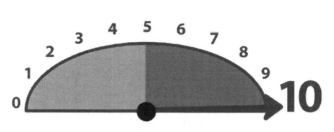

BECAUSE BARK LEADS TO BITE

Refuse to fight dirty. One of the scariest, most volatile kinds of men is the kind who can't control his anger. If a guy can't stop himself from punching walls, getting into barfights, or saying gratuitously awful things to you or anyone else —family and friends, for example — something is very wrong with him. Who knows where his rage comes from and who cares! For your strongest self, anger management issues are an instant deal killer. She knows that the sexiest men have self-control. They communicate like healthy adults, no matter how heated the battle. If you find yourself with a guy who doesn't fight fair, run in the other direction. Fast. You can't save him, only a professional can.

Dream big. Being with a man who's occasionally mean to you is a red flag that you've lost your way. And that's okay, as long as you stop, give yourself a reality check, and self-correct. Finding a special someone isn't exactly easy and most of us kiss a lot of frogs along the way. If that sounds familiar, don't be ashamed to admit it. And don't be afraid to walk away. Any relationship worth having should make you feel stronger than if you were just on your own. Ask yourself: Does your guy bring out the best in you? Does he make you feel like twice the woman or does he cut you down to size? Bad guys are notorious for reducing your self-worth to the point where you believe you can't survive without them. That's a myth abusers like to perpetuate. It's how they stay in business. But you know better. Remember the fairy tales you once believed in? It's time to rekindle their magic. Sure, a hot prince on a sturdy white steed isn't going to gallop up Main Street to rescue you but we say, hey, a girl can dream. That doesn't mean you should cling to crazy fantasies – but there is something to be said for believing in romance and looking for a partner who brings it into your life.

****

He Can't Stop Talking About Other Women

Evan and I have been seeing each other for a year. When we first started dating, he had an annoying habit: He would talk about other women to try to make me jealous. He would tell me about some girl who hit on him when he was out the night before or remind me how hot his ex was. It was obnoxious, but I let it go because it was also transparent — I could tell he was trying to impress me. Now, we've been dating for a while and he still does the same thing. He'll tell me about this girl he works with that has a crush on him or, when we get into a fight, he'll say something like there are a million women dying to date him. When's it going to stop?

A million women, huh? Wow. That's some serious game. So how come he's such an insecure asshole?

Lots of guys, when they really like a girl, try to impress her with subtle (and sometimes not-so-subtle) comments suggesting that hoards of hot women lust after them. It's as if they're on a job interview and they want to seem invaluable and in demand. Like male peacocks during a mating dance, they're just shaking their tail feathers hoping to grab your, er, attention. Assuming it's just that, it can be kinda endearing.

But it's not at all flattering in Evan's case. Because he is not flirting or trying to impress you, he's threatening you. He's essentially saying, "If you don't [insert blackmail activity here], I'll leave you for one of legions of ladies who would kill to date me."

Anyone who negotiates with his partner in this way, undermining her sense of security in the relationship (and eventually, possibly, marriage), is not mature enough to be in a couple. You should tell Evan that while there might be a million women after him, you're definitely not one of them.

And the Asshole Meter says:

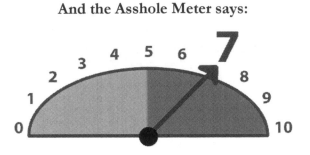

BECAUSE TALKING ABOUT OTHER WOMEN IS TACKY AND MEAN

Don't fall for the "I've got so many better options" B.S. Being in a relationship shouldn't feel like a test. If your guy likes to keep you on your toes by demanding that you prove yourself every few days, lest he leave you for some other girl, he's just an asshole. Your strongest self knows that one of the biggest perks of being in a couple is the security you feel from having a partner you can depend on. And that doesn't work if your partner makes you feel like he might leave at any second. Don't leave his dependability to chance. Leave now. Before he becomes a self-fulfilling prophecy.

Never worry about the other woman. If you're in a relationship and feel concerned or threatened by someone else, something's not right. Turn the mirror back on yourself for a moment. You'll likely see your weakest self staring you in the face. Kick her out the door and let your strongest self take over. She's in touch with her gifts and knows she's a special catch. She knows that your desirability comes from the very fact that you believe in yourself without question and don't need to prove anything to anyone. She'll never let you compare yourself to, or compete with, another woman for the attention of a man. That's a losing proposition. So if a guy ever expects you to do either, set him free and let someone from his fan club play his game.

****

He's a Control Freak

My boyfriend Nate really loves me, almost too much. The thought of us not being together freaks him out, so much so that he can be a little paranoid sometimes. He doesn't think I'm cheating, but he worries that I might find someone else so he kinda watches me when we're out. More than once, he's come looking for me when I've gone to the ladies room. And he often thinks guys are hitting on me when they're not so he hates it if I'm friendly to a waiter or bartender. We've had a lot of fights over him thinking I was flirting and he even called me a slut once. That was really hurtful, but I also know he didn't mean it. He was just scared. We've definitely had some rough moments but overall, I know he loves me. So I'm trying to be better about not upsetting him, hoping he'll become more secure over time.

You're not Nate's girlfriend. You're his little puppy. And he's trying to train you.

In a healthy, loving relationship, a woman can go pee by herself without her boyfriend feeling like he needs to check up on her. She can be friendly with the bartender and not be accused of flirting. And her boyfriend isn't easily threatened, needing to call her a slut to hide his own insecurities and keep her in check.

What Nate feels for you, on the other hand, isn't love, it's a sense of ownership. He doesn't respect you as a person, but sees you as an object to be controlled. And it's the guys who think of women as belonging to them that often turn into the stalkers, abusers and even killers.

The problem with Nate is that he isn't a confident guy. He's pretty sure you'll eventually leave him. To prevent that from happening, he's trying to tear you down and make you dependent on him. He slowly introduces rules for what you can and can't do and when you break them, he calls you names to make you feel bad. But then he quickly apologizes and gives you a treat (Good girl! Woof!). This way, you start to need him to feel good. His goal: to make you feel so small that you'll be powerless to disobey him or leave him.

So kick that controlling asshole to the curb. If you don't, you'll end up a pale version of yourself or worse: maybe even dead.

And the Asshole Meter says:

BECAUSE A RELATIONSHIP SHOULDN'T KEEP YOU ON A TIGHT LEASH

Don't confuse control with love. The stronger the connection in your relationship, the greater the freedom you're supposed to experience. You're free to take risks because you're supported by your partner, free to make your own decisions because you've built trust, free to be yourself because you're loved unconditionally. If you're in a relationship that's making you feel caged, you're dating a control freak and quite possibly a psycho. No guy should ever police your pee time or monitor you're mingling. If he needs to do that to feel secure, he's got a problem. Don't prove you're also a head case by going along with his behavior. Listen to your strongest self and fly away!

CHAPTER SEVEN

The Guy Who Has an Unhealthy Relationship to Sex

He Won't Glove His Love

I've been seeing Eric for a few weeks. I'm reeaally into him and the sex is unbelievable. The one thing that sorta stresses me out is that we never use condoms. I want to, and almost always do, but he hates them. He used one the first couple of times we had sex but since then, he always weasels his way out of it. And now, I feel like, what's the point? I'm on the pill, so I'm not getting pregnant. And if he had anything, I would've seen the signs by now so he's probably clean. So, I might as well enjoy it, right?

You're playing penis roulette. And you should be more careful. Because those things are loaded.

If Eric isn't wrapping his rod with you, he sure as hell isn't laying rubber with other women. The likelihood that he's walking around with some kind of sexually transmitted disease is pretty high. That's not rocket science.

What is far less obvious is why you're willing to be this guy's ongoing STD test. Who knows if he's ever been tested or how often and what those results might have been. What is clear is that the only way you'll know if he has something, is by seeing whether you get it. Ouch. That's like waiting for your head to crash through a windshield before deciding you need to wear a seatbelt. And rather than telling this host monkey to go to hell for pressuring you into that position, you're content to keep sleeping with him, repeatedly risking your safety as he does God-knows-what with countless whoevers. Do the math – how many people he could be sleeping with and how many people those women are sleeping with, and so on and so on – and the numbers go viral (pun intended) very quickly. Like we said, you're like his annual health exam: every time he has sex with you, he might as well pee into a little cup.

STDs are dangerous, and can wreak all sorts of havoc on a body. True, you have no idea if Eric is infected. For all you know, he isn't right now, but he might pick up a little something special tonight, before you sleep with him tomorrow.

To be clear: We love us some sex. But no guy has given us an orgasm worth a lifetime of painful sores and itching. An irresponsible asshole who not only doesn't care about his own health, but is also willing to jeopardize yours, isn't worth the risk. Quit while you're ahead: Tell Eric that the lab experiments are over and his genital petri dish can breed bacteria in someone else's bed.

And the Asshole Meter says:

BECAUSE CONDOMS ARE THE COST OF ENTRY

Demand respect in the bedroom. Your body is, indeed, a temple and, if a guy wants to enter, he better treat your vag like the paradise it is. Your strongest self knows that being with you is an honor and a gift. During sex, she expects to feel relished and respected, not made to feel like a receptacle or a tool. So if a dick shows up to her door entitled, dirty, or bareback ... entry denied!

Protect yourself. Sex is all fun and games until someone gets genital hurties or crotch crickets. While getting down and dirty with a hot guy has its upsides, your strongest self knows that sex is also a very serious act that carries serious risks, especially for women. While everyone is vulnerable to STDs, women are more susceptible than men, not to mention suffer the most from an unplanned pregnancy. Next time a guy tries to push his poker in without a poncho, slam those legs shut until he comes correct. An awkward moment only lasts a minute but the anxiety from wondering "what if" lasts a lot longer and, more important: You could be left dealing with the effects of your choice — babies or blisters, for starters — for the rest of your life.

****

He Won't Stop When It Hurts

My boyfriend Stephen and I are super turned on by each other. So, obviously the sex is great. Sometimes, though, he gets a little carried away with the thrusting and doesn't realize that it hurts me. I'll start to pull away and tighten up, but he doesn't seem to notice so I tell him and, even then, he doesn't seem to fully get it. The last couple of times, he slowed down for a few seconds and then just went back at it. Later, when I brought it up, he said I was being too sensitive. I don't know, am I?

Stephen needs sex lessons. Lesson one: When your woman tells you that what you're doing is causing her pain, quit it. Duh.

Jackhammering is not an uncommon tendency. A lot of men do it and many men can't have an orgasm without repeatedly thrusting fast and hard. It can feel good for us but often – particularly if a guy isn't paying attention to the force he's using, like Stephen – it can be quite painful. Lube helps but nothing is better than communication. If your man cares about you, he'll appreciate being educated about how his thrusting feels and he'll respond by slowing things down to a rhythm that feels good for both of you. Hopefully, he'll discover that he doesn't need to pound you to get off and that, in fact, an orgasm that comes from slower movements that you both take the time to really feel and appreciate can be a lot more powerful (and can build a much deeper connection).

So, we suggest you have a proper conversation with Stephen. Warmly bring up the topic after your next love session ends and see how he responds. If he continues focusing on himself, pull up those panties and start walking. After all, your boyfriend essentially hijacking your cooch to rub one out isn't good sex. If you want to experience heaven between the sheets, you need a man who understands that your vag is a privilege, not a punching bag.

And the Asshole Meter says:

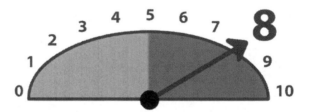

BECAUSE "OUCH THAT HURTS" ISN'T A CUE TO GO HARDER

Define "mindblowing sex" by what feels good to both of you. When you're in sync with your man, you *both* innately move to fulfill each other's needs — the connection feels seamless and powerful. An other-worldly sexual experience is impossible to achieve when you're with a guy who doesn't care about your basic comfort level. Your strongest self knows that sex will never be memorable with a man who's not trying to make it feel great for you. And isn't that just another way of saying that he's bad in bed? You deserve more than that. You deserve great sex.

****

He's Thinks His Morning Dry Hump is Foreplay

Peter and I met a couple of months ago and immediately hit it off. Things have been awesome between us, but I've noticed lately that, most of the time we have sex, it's in the morning. And there's rarely foreplay. I get woken up by him pushing his penis up against me and then he pulls me on top. I know a lot of guys prefer morning sex, but why should he wake me up just to do all the work?

What you and Peter are doing is so one-sided, it almost doesn't sound like sex. It sounds more like masturbation — where you're the hand. And we're willing to bet a few bucks that Peter's one of those guys who not-so-subtly pushes your head south when he's in the mood for some a.m. head. Hey, we hear it's better than coffee.

Wtf.

Peter is an asshole. Two months into a relationship, you should *both* be super hot for each other, excited and eager to explore your needs and bodies. Instead, Peter's checked out like a fat man on a Lazy Boy. He's not interested in building something meaningful with you. If he were, he'd ask what pleases you, rather than use you as a vibrating inflatable doll.

Don't kill the messenger, but it's not all Peter's fault. The less you respect yourself, the more Peter will treat you like an object and use you as his personal sex slave. And you are the only person who can put an end to that. Hopefully, the next man you meet will be motivated not just to receive, but to give too.

And the Asshole Meter says:

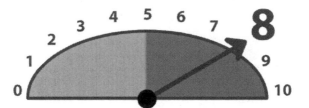

BECAUSE ALL TAKE AND NO GIVE IS NOT OKAY

Just say no to bad sex. Getting laid is not always fantastic, but it shouldn't always suck either. If you'd rather do your laundry than do your man, because he's all about his own needs, move on. You might try to convince yourself that a little somethin' is better than nothing, but that's self-defeating nonsense. Your strongest self knows that the emptiness you feel after being with a guy who isn't interested in fulfilling your sexual needs — physical and emotional — is far worse than being alone. (We see your man and raise you a six-pack of AAs and a box of Rabbits — at least you don't have to do all the work.) A guy who chooses not to give and receive is, frankly, a waste of time.

****

He's a Premature Sexter

I recently met this guy, James, who is super cute, successful, and fun. We've gone out twice and have hooked up, but haven't slept together. That might be this weekend! I'm excited to move things to the next level, but he did something after our last date that left me a little unsettled. He texted the next morning, "I'm getting hard just thinking about you." I wasn't sure what to make of that. Was he trying to have phone sex? Or just trying to tell me he's into me? I eventually just replied with a smiley face and nothing else. Later that night, he texted me again: I can't wait to fuck you." I was weirded out, and a little turned off. But maybe I'm a prude. I like him, I'm totally attracted to him, and I do want to sleep with him. Should I just write him back something dirty next time?

You might want to hold off on having sex with James. Because sex with James would probably be like sex with Stephen (from the chapter on painful sex) — repeated, aggressive thrusting down your manhole. Hardhat not included.

James doesn't understand what turns a woman on. If he did, he would wait until you both were more comfortable with each other and had shared some physical intimacy before trying to sext with you. And, hopefully, if you did reach that point, he would stifle his Talk Dirty Tourettes and be a bit more careful, starting off slowly, watching how you respond and changing course as needed.

Instead, James is doing whatever gets him off, without regard for how you might react, nor any sense as to what's socially acceptable. All James cares about is the fantasy he's created of you two in his head, whether or not you care to be in it.

James may or may not be just an asshole. He might just be painfully clueless and in need of some guidance from a woman he trusts. Either way, we don't think premature sexting is hot, and hopefully you don't either. Because there's a good chance that the next text you get is an up-close shot of his penis. And no amount of airbrushing can make that cute.

And the Asshole Meter says:

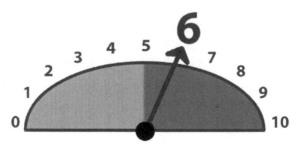

BECAUSE IF YOU'RE NOT HAVING SEX, YOU SHOULDN'T BE HAVING SEXT

Look for sound judgment. It's normal to be enthusiastic (read: horny) in a new relationship, but if a guy fast-forwards to whatever turns him on, before you've given him the green light, something's wrong with him. Sure, he might just not be good at reading the signs, or perhaps he's too self-involved to spot your signals. Either way, your strongest self is just not that into him. She doesn't want to get pounced when she's having a conversation. She doesn't want a tongue down her throat when she's moving in for a peck. And she doesn't want a hand up her skirt during a simple kiss. A respectful guy behaves like a gentleman, even when he wants to tear your skirt off. He exercises good judgment because he's waiting for you to set the pace. He thinks before he acts, reading your cues like a map. The result: a great start to what's hopefully a great relationship.

✳✳✳✳✳✳✳✳✳

He's a Porn Dog

My boyfriend, Chris, watches a lot of porn. He didn't used to when we first met, but he acquired a taste after we watched something together one night. Since then, he watches it alone (he doesn't know I know this) and his sex drive has diminished. When we do have sex, he tries to get me into all sorts of funky positions like I'm a porn star. It's a little annoying. Should I be worried?

You know how you wish your boyfriend would look and act like the leading man in [insert romantic comedy du jour here] — the boy next door who was nice, but a little bit bad, and loyal, and hot, and charming and funny, and successful, with six pack abs, a great sense of style and endearing mannerisms that made him sweet but also wildly sexy in bed?

Yeah, those characters are definitely pretty awesome (we'd love us some Ryan Gosling or, hell, any one of Blake Lively's hand-me-downs) but sigh … they don't exist in the real world. They're make believe. Fantasy. Fake. And if you actually expected your boyfriend to behave like those characters, you'd be, more or less, an idiot. Because no matter how badly you want your guy to serenade you under a balcony, he probably ain't gonna.

Similarly, if your boyfriend actually expects you to want to watch porn with him all the time and enjoy having cum shot in your eyeball, he's an idiot. Because porn stars aren't real either. They're actually paid to lick a guy's asshole. We'd bet they wouldn't if they weren't on the clock.

Chris's problem is that his ability to enjoy normal sex, i.e, sex that is not just about getting off, but also about sharing intimacy with a normal woman — one who has a little cellulite and can't bend herself into a pretzel — is being destroyed by his porn-heightened expectations. Sex is not just about the body, but also the mind, and his brain is getting rewired such that it only responds to extreme XXX situations.

If you care about Chris, have a serious conversation

with him about how his T&A habit is making you feel, the toll it's taking on your relationship, and the concern you feel for him. If he cares about you more than his new hobby, you'll sense that and the two of you can work on the problem together. If he doesn't get it, he's not necessarily an asshole, but he might as well be to you.

And the Asshole Meter says:

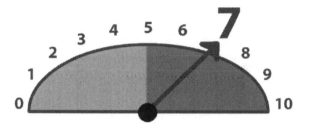

BECAUSE BEING A FLUFFER SUCKS

Watch out for the super freaks. People have all sorts of different turn-ons when it comes to the bedroom, some more peculiar than others. And supportive partners often help each other live out their harmless fantasies. If your guy wants you to dress up like Smurfette, that's a little weird, but whatevs! No downside in giving him what he's hot for. Unless, of course, he just can't get off anymore until you paint yourself cobalt blue. Your strongest self knows that while it's good to mix it up in the bedroom (or bathroom or kitchen …), sex is mostly about expressing love and affection for your partner. If that gets lost because your dude is only focused on the end result or his athletic prowess along the way, he's not capable of satisfying you. Truly satisfying, earth-shattering sex happens only when two people are focused on each other's needs, not just their own.

****

He Wants to Double His Pleasure

Adam, my boyfriend of two years has been asking me recently if I'm open to bringing a woman into our bedroom, just as an experiment. I wasn't totally surprised because he's always said that girl-on-girl action is hot. Problem is that I'm not into it … I don't think it's such an awful thing, but I have no interest in kissing a girl or watching him kiss another girl. I told him that when he brought it up again last night and he said fine, but I could tell he was annoyed. He made some comment about how I may want to be a little more adventurous. I didn't reply, hoping this would just go away. Or maybe I should just do it?

Here's an idea: Ask Adam if, just as an experiment, he can stop acting like an asshole.

You're not unadventurous just because the idea of watching your boyfriend have sex with another woman doesn't appeal to you. Some women may enjoy that, but a lot of women would feel cheated upon – which is so not hot – and are therefore horrified by the concept.

We know that a lot of guys fantasize about having threesomes — that's not unusual. Some guys, taking the conservative approach, hint at the idea to see how their girlfriends react. Others will boldly ask, possibly jeopardizing their relationship if their girlfriend gets skeeved. And still others, like Adam, will virtually insist on it as they try to bully you into it, which is completely unacceptable, totally offensive, and should make you run screaming out the door.

Adam's priorities are all wrong and, if you stay with him, you'll see more and more signs of that. This is a guy who's willing to risk your feelings, self-respect, confidence in the relationship, and its integrity for a sexual fantasy that he just can't seem to keep to himself. We believe sex (including fun, adventurous sex) is an important part of any healthy relationship, but any guy who acts like it's *the* most important part is not just an asshole, he's also a little shallow.

If Adam really wants to have sex with another girl, we think you should let him. Once you've kicked his ass out the door.

And the Asshole Meter says:

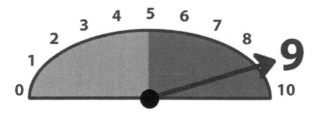

BECAUSE THREE'S A CROWD

Don't get bullied in the bedroom. Bullying is awful no matter where it takes place. And one of the worst places for someone to manipulate or assert control is the bedroom. Your strongest self won't stand for it. She believes healthy sex requires trust between two people and she's immediately suspicious of any guy who abuses that trust by trying to browbeat her into something she's uncomfortable with. If some selfish guy says she's "unadventurous" just because she's not into something he wants to try, she doesn't suddenly second-guess her prowess when it comes to pleasure. She knows that bullies will say anything to get what they want and she's too smart to listen. So follow her lead, trust yourself above all else, and head right out the door.

****

He's Obs-ASS-ed

My boyfriend, Nick, and I have a pretty comfortable relationship. We've been together for two years and, to spice things up, I finally agreed to do anal. It's not something I really wanted to do, but I did it for him. It wasn't as bad as I thought it would be, but I also didn't enjoy it. Afterward, I was a good sport and let him do it another five or six times. Now, I'm over it. I don't want to do it again. I told him that and he wasn't happy. And then, the next few times we had sex, he brought it up again, trying to coax me into it in the heat of the moment. I gave in a couple more times and the times I didn't give in, he kept "accidentally" poking my ass. I love Nick but I don't ever want to have to do it again. Am I being selfish?

Nick's not an asshole because he likes assholes; he might be, though, if he can't get past the fact that you're not into anal.

Anal sex is no longer the taboo it once was, especially when both parties are comfortable and open-minded enough to discuss it. That doesn't mean, however, that everyone has to try it or enjoy it. The backdoor wasn't your thing, but in the interest of compromise and making your boyfriend happy, you gave it a shot.

Don't feel pressured into believing this is something you need to do for your guy. Despite Nick's protests, anal isn't necessarily an acquired taste, and like with most bedroom activities, a guy needs to follow a little etiquette and, in this case, some prep work. For instance, "oops, sorry, wrong hole" is never Miss Manners-approved, nor is coercing someone mid-sex or surprising her with a sneak (crack) attack. Bad manners are one of the quickest ways to get bounced out of a woman's bed.

If Nick wants anal love, it's his turn to bend a little — he needs to show you that he values you for more than just your backdoor by honoring what pleases both of you. If he refuses to respect your boundaries, strut that butt out the door.

And the Asshole Meter says:

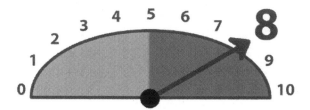

BECAUSE YOUR BOUNDARIES ARE TO BE RESPECTED

Establish and enforce boundaries. Sure, compromise is important in a relationship, but there's a big difference between mutually agreeable exploration and finding a dick shoved up your ass after you've said no. It's your responsibility to be clear about your rules and his job to respect them. It's also up to you to be willing to leave someone who consistently violates them. When you set limits about what feels safe and acceptable to you in bed, and then allow your partner to thrust his manhood right over the line, you're compromising your self-respect for a minute or two of his pleasure. Doesn't sound like a fair trade-off to us. Honor yourself first by understanding what works for your body and articulating that to your guy. Let him know that attempts to sneak into your backdoor after you've clearly said "access denied" won't work for you anymore. If he can't keep his cock in check, give it a well-deserved time out or find a man who can.

CONCLUSION

Congratulations! You've finished the book. So, now what?

If you're dating a guy who resembles one of the assholes we just covered, you know what must be done: It's time to become your strongest self and tell that guy to hit the road!

It's the right thing to do.

In fact, as we've discussed over the last seven chapters, your future depends on it. If you want a fantastic guy in your life, you have to start acting like you deserve to be respected and treated well. That means no longer hanging out with mediocre men who don't make you happy. No more wasting time on bad guys and fools. You know what you want from a relationship, and you're no longer interested in men who aren't focused on giving it to you. It's that simple.

And if you're single, get ready to mingle!

Hopefully, we've helped to remind you that there's a standard by which a woman should be treated. And when you have clarity around how men should behave with you, dating becomes far less complicated and way more fun. Because you're good at weeding out the assholes, the amazing guys that do exist become much easier to see.

So get out there and find yourself a good man. That's why we wrote a book about assholes: To help you live a life free of them!

And don't forget to visit us on the web at www.TheAholeBook.com. We have some good stuff coming so give us your email address and we'll let you know when there's new stuff to check out!

Finally, if you liked the book, please leave us a review! We'd be super grateful. Thanks!

INDEX

Chapter One

Recognize bullshit when you see it.   7

Never negotiate the basics.   8

Send it back, if it's not what you ordered.   10

Don't be distracted by the package.   12

Date men, not boys.   14

Remember that men are "as is".   14

Chapter Two

Expect to be a priority, not an option.   17

Stop wondering whether he's into you.   18

Snuff out old flames.   20

Don't be a sitting duck.   21

Look forward, not back.   24

Recalibrate.   24

Don't settle for flashes of goodness.   26

Don't pretend sex doesn't matter.   29

Delay gratification.   29

Chapter Three

Remember, you're the objective.   33

Don't waste your youth thinking you're old.   34

Banish insecurity from your life.   36

Rock what yo mama gave you.   37

Know your deal breakers.   40

Chapter Four

Put it through the sniff test.   44

Walk if it's not developing organically.   44

Walk if you want to win.   47

Play like you have a weak hand and you'll   47
lose, every time.

Steer clear of self-proclaimed losers.   50

Don't get sucked into the vortex of   51
someone else's misery.

Never go dutch.   51

Notice his choices.   54

Keep your life full.   54

When a guy tells you who he is, listen.   57

Chapter Five

Know your worth.   60

Look at his actions, not his excuses.   60

Refuse to be an afterthought.   63

Don't reward bad behavior.   64

Don't forgive a cheater.   66

Follow your gut when something feels off.   67

Expect intimacy.   69

Express your preferences.   69

Look at how his last relationship ended.   72

Steer clear of secret keepers.   72

Beware of brazen assholes.   75

Pay attention to the small lies.   75

Ditch mystery men.   77

Chapter Six

Avoid guys with excessive ego.   80

Never minimize your accomplishments.   80

Refuse to fight dirty.   83

Dream big.   83

Don't fall for the "I've got so many   86
better options" B.S.

Never worry about the other woman.   86

Don't confuse control with love.   89

Chapter Seven

Demand respect in the bedroom.   92

Protect yourself.   92

Define "mindblowing sex" by what feels   94
good to both of you.

Just say no to bad sex.   96

Look for sound judgment.   99

Watch out for the super freaks.   101

Don't get bullied in the bedroom.   104

Establish and enforce rock-solid   106
boundaries.

Made in the USA
San Bernardino, CA
08 April 2016